"We all have a cabin in memory. Our dream cabin. The little place where the family vacationed when we were young. Though they may look much different from north to south, mountains to fields, there's something special about cabins, something that sets them apart from small houses . . . it is the gold mine of memories that really defines the cabin."

Dale Mulfinger and Susan Davis in *The Cabin*

D1545871

John Henricksson

THE
GUNFLINT CABIN

A Northwoods Memoir

Beaver's Pond Press

ISBN 10: 1-59298-219-0
ISBN 13: 978-1-59298-219-6

Library of Congress Control Number: 2001012345
Printed in the United States of America
First Printing, February 2008
Second Printing, November 2008
11 10 09 08   6 5 4 3 2

Beaver's Pond Press is an imprint of
Beaver's Pond Group
7104 Ohms Lane, Suite 101
Edina, Minnesota, 55439-2129
www.beaverspondpress.com

Cover Woodcut by Betsy Bowen

To those great-hearted fire crews, volunteers and emergency personnel who fought the 2007 Ham Lake wildfire, Minnesota's largest and most destructive forest fire of the past century. They saved most of this upper Gunflint Trail neighborhood and earned the gratitude and respect of everyone.

Contents

ACKNOWLEDGMENTS

Essentially, this is a book about a remote neighborhood in a region of lakes, rivers and a sub-boreal forest and the people who are bound here by the love of this land. We are year-round residents, vacationers, seasonal residents and week-enders. There are a few big homes, but the great majority of dwellings are still traditional family cabins. The anecdotes, knowledge, gossip, folk wisdom and perceptions all come from years of visiting with these neighbors, so the first low bow must be to them. It is their book.

Then there are the very necessary people who can answer the Who, What, Why, When and Where questions the writer must ask to put some meat on his story's bones. Sue McDonnell, Orville Gilmore, Sharlene LeTourneau, Debbie Mark, Katie Lush, Vera Flavel, Vi Nelson, Ken Rusk, Ardis David, Mike and Kathy Lande, Larry and Sue Schei, Bruce and Sue Kerfoot could all be relied on for the different perspectives of life on the Gunflint.

Chief Curator and Head of Collections, Marcia Anderson, and the librarians of film and print material at the Minnesota Historical Society were always ready to help with their unique knowledge and resources. Pat

Zankman, Director of the Cook County Historical Society, opened her photo files and data bases whenever I needed help. Silviculturist Myra Theimer, and wildlife biologist Lissa Grover of the U.S. Forest Service at the Gunflint Ranger Station in Grand Marais, provided much necessary information on the new Gunflint forest and its wildlife.

I also must acknowledge author Richard Louv and his publisher Algonquin Books for their permission to use generously from Louv's book *Last Child in the Woods* in Chapter 10. Julie Henricksson, Betsy Bowen, Barbara Halowell and Pam McClanahan provided frequent and useful editorial advice and I am grateful to all of them.

THE FAMILY CABIN— AN ENDANGERED SPECIES?

IN THIS WORLD OF DAZZLING CHANGES in transportation, economics, technology and the work ethic, the setting and the concepts of leisure time activities and destinations have all combined to push that Minnesota icon, the old family cabin up at the lake, out into the murky dusk of the threatened species list. In recent years, thousands of them have fallen before bulldozer blades to be replaced by larger more expensive homes, townhouses and condos because the property they sit on is usually very desirable lakefront. That cabin, seldom grand or imposing, has been a treasure of more than two million Minnesota families for over a century. The cabin experience has always been the talisman of solitude, recreation and beauty; that totem place which always lingers, just in sight, beckoning at the edge of stressful cauldrons—a sanctuary, a family bond and often the owner's signature.

Shortly before this book went off to the publisher, the neighbor lady, who knew I was writing a book about cabins, brought over a wonderful little privately published book called *Betty Bear's Family Secrets*. She had gone to high school with Betty Bear and they had remained in sometimes touch for 60 years and Betty sent her a copy when it was published in 2000. *Family Secrets*, fifty years in the writing, is primarily a book of recipes and remembrances and is written with an artless, informal eloquence that sometimes blossoms from the pens of memoir writers. Betty Bear has captured perfectly the ambience of, and the feelings for, the Minnesota family cabin:

The Little Red Cabin by Betty Bear

"It was a hot, humid night and Dave couldn't sleep. We were visiting our parents in the Twin Cities for a couple of weeks on our way to an assignment at Fort Benning, Georgia.

"Dave had been checking real estate ads and decided to drive north in the early morning hours through a heavy rain. He remembers walking down the hill of Mogensen's Shores at first light with trees dripping overhead, and there he found a small red cabin by the lake. What a gigantic part of our family's memories have taken place at that cabin on South Long Lake near Brainerd. It was purchased in the summer of 1960, and those were "cabin days," when families were content to spend their vacations in a primitive environment. We were tired of going from house to house for meals and small talk whenever we returned to Minnesota on leave. We wanted a place of our own where our children could swim, Dave could fish and friends could come and visit and relax. The cabin was just a shell with 100 feet of shoreline and thousands of moths inside, but Dave came back to St. Paul and announced he had found our cabin. The cost was $2,250, including a boat and motor. It took us three years to pay for it.

"For our family the cabin has become home and has given our children Minnesota roots even though we spent more than another decade moving to various army posts in the U.S. and overseas. Summers, when possible, I would journey back to South Long Lake with our children. We would fish, swim, hike, read and spend most of our waking hours outdoors. Dave was usually able to join us for a couple of weeks.

"During the early 1960s Dave and Grandpa Knute worked diligently at paneling walls and making other improvements. We started out with an outdoor pump, a clothesline for drying swimsuits and we cooked on a Coleman stove . . . My dad got some old screens and a screen house was built for cleaning fish.

"Those summers we played hundreds of games of cribbage and put together countless jigsaw puzzles. We played cards with my parents and the Olsens, Hannah and Ben, who had a cabin next door. They never cut their grass and Mrs. Olsen would take Beth and Amy hunting for agates and wild flowers. Mrs. Hippe lived up the hill and down the road were Mary Mogenson, the Handelands and the Albertsons. Mary had eyes like little stars and she loved to come down for coffee and donuts soon as we arrived. She stitched a quilt for each of our children before she died.

"My thoughts take me back to many summers in the Red Cabin. I recall thunderstorms, waves whipping up on the beach and falling trees. I remember decorating the outhouse, cold and rainy June days when Beth was tucked away in her bunk reading and Amy was off playing with

Kathie Handeland . . . Of course, the main event whenever we were at the Red Cabin was always fishing and Grandpa Knute and Dave brought in stringers full of bass and pails of sunfish and crappies . . . On the porch you'll find fishing tackle, life jackets and outboard motors while all the other rooms are crowded with boxes for the next garage sale. However if you look closely, you will see it is still filled with memories: the bunk beds Beth and Amy slept in, shelves filled with games, puzzles and childrens' books. There's an old wood stove and a bulletin board 35-years old.

"The pages of our guest book tell many colorful stories and bring back thoughts of our visitors over the years; friends and relations who came from Ohio, New Hampshire, Oregon, New Jersey, California, Michigan, Arizona and from as far away as Germany, Sweden, England, Finland and Japan.

"Some things at the Red Cabin will never change. There will always be boats to bail, mosquitoes, an occasional skunk, some deer and, oh yes, fish to clean. What kept bringing us back are the memories of warm days, cool nights, early morning fishing and glorious sunsets. It's a place we have always come to to regenerate our lives from the busy world around us. The Red Cabin is part of a dream Dave built—after seeing it that first misty morning in 1960, and we've all been fortunate to come here to play, relax and grow as a family."

Jeff Forester, writing for the Lakeshore and Recreational Property Owners newsletter, *The Update*, applauds traditional values and explains the peculiar affinity Minnesotans feel with their cabins:

"Minnesotans are cabin people. Many of us were raised on a lake. I was. The lake place defines my family, and so largely defines me. It gives a context to our lives . . . cabins give Minnesotans a cornerstone. We know where we come from and, like salmon, we instinctively find our way back to our beginnings. Cabins are where family happens in Minnesota.

"Each time we return, we honor the little rustic places that define us, that lead to our self-reliance, our folksiness, our love of nature. Life in a cabin breeds Minnesota values of family, hard work, frontier skills, boatsmanship and humility. Minnesotans do not like those who put on airs, and probably much of this has to do with our collective familiarity with outhouses, woodpiles, leeches and ticks. So, here's to the clapboard and cedar log places tucked back into wooded lots around the state. Cabins are a habitat that need protection."

But we have become a society of more urban and suburban interests now and our vastly different lifestyles are creating an altered state which is reflected in our choice of vacation homes. Considering these trends, architect/author Dale Mulfinger speaking on "Cabinology" at the Voices in the Valley forum in Stillwater, Minnesota, said, "We have a rich legacy of family cabins in Minnesota. They are mostly very modest structures; 'just a cabin' is a Minnesota term. When you put a deck and a two-car garage on it, it is no longer a cabin. Our grandchildren will probably not even know what a cabin is."

Current vacation-home builders require a grander venue than the three-room cabin, outdoor biffy and a fishing boat that started it all. Even the word "cabin" seems to be out of vogue now. It is seldom used any more by developers. They call them vacation homes and recreational properties now. Not all the development and redevelopment is bad, of course, but the new elaborate expansions are changing the landscape radically.

Unless a severe economic downturn, a shutdown of the oil pumps or some other recessional disaster occurs, it appears the condominium-townhouse-megahouse type development will eventually spread statewide. Presently it is the region centered around Brainerd which has seen the most dramatic transformation. Chris Williams, writing in the *St. Paul Pioneer Press*, noted that:

"In most places in Minnesota, $1.6 million buys the nicest house on the block. The Central Lakes region of Minnesota is no longer one of those places. There has been an explosive re-development of this six county region in the past ten years that has seen hundreds of people replacing rustic lake cabins with large houses."

There are pockets of traditional cabin country left in some of the more remote areas of the state, such as the northeastern part of the Arrowhead region, where our Gunflint cabin neighborhood is located. Gunflint is backcountry, far from the city and not yet affected too much by suburban development, but much of the North Shore of Lake Superior, just to the south of the Gunflint region, is also beginning to take on a bedroom community, suburban appearance. All, that is, except the Grand Portage Indian Reservation at the very tip of the Arrowhead, the most beautiful chunk of North Shore left. Curtis Gagnon, trust administrator for the band of Ojibwe which own this land and is buying up available properties in the area with proceeds from their casino, recently told writer Greg Breining in an article for *Minnesota Monthly* magazine:

"I guess the band has been looking at what has been happening up and down the shore—all the development, the huge encroachments, people building fabulous homes, and huge cabins . . . and they wanted something for the generations to come, for people to enjoy what we enjoy today."

With travel ease and improvements, the expansion of things to do with vacation time such as the theme parks, luxury resorts, water parks, golf courses, historical and wildlife tours, ecotourism, and the hundreds of activities found on the Internet, the old cabin may no longer get a very high priority in the vacation plans of many families. Also the family's much greater mobility makes the national parks, foreign countries, new cultures and new attractions easily available.

There is another and often overlooked reason for letting the traditional time at the cabin slip this year, and that is a big change in the work ethic. Time was when cabin time meant work time. There was always a new porch or bedroom to build, a new dock to put in, a woodpile to split and stack, a new water system to install, a leaky roof to patch or replace. Cabin time almost always involved one or more work projects. People don't seem to enjoy that working vacation much anymore. The packaged vacations offered almost anyplace in the world today require nothing more than arriving and enjoying.

Perhaps most important, there are strong economic

temptations for cabin owners selling out to a new generation. Middle income families and fixed income retirees, who have made up the great majority of Minnesota cabin owners, watch anxiously as their taxes increase when neighbors on either side sell their cabin properties for prices undreamed of 20 years ago. As a result, estimated market values climb, so the cabin property, representing now a glorious and unexpected windfall as well as a rapidly escalating tax burden, often is sold.

Considering the grim future of the traditional and much-loved family cabin, it might be appropriate now, for the historical record, that an old cabin owner chronicle the joys and appeal of wild nature, grand times, true neighborhoods and also some of the problems of life "up at the cabin." Older readers will probably say, "Oh yeah, I remember that." And the younger ones, if they occasionally long for a different and simpler lifestyle, may say, "Hey, cool."

Chapter 1

THE CABIN CHARISMA

TO MANY THE CABIN MEANS SOLITUDE, absolute and continuous solitude. Several writers have spoken about their longing and need for the solitude of the cabin. Henry David Thoreau, Anne Morrow Lindbergh, Eugene O'Neill, Sherwood Anderson, Calvin Rutstrum, Arthur Miller, Helen Hoover, and many others, were among writers who preferred to work in the solitude of their cabins. Sig Olson wrote at length about the wonderful solitude of Listening Point, his cabin on Burntside Lake, near Ely, Minnesota. Others see the cabin as a playground for the extended family, and the whooping and hollering of children is constantly heard from the dock and in the surrounding woods. The cabin should be whatever the owners want it to be. A place to retreat, a place to socialize, a place to work or to rest, or whatever. The key to the cabin is renewal of body and spirit.

Most family cabins are "up to the lake," but there are many on rivers, on the open prairie or in the deep woods, in clusters or in lonely places—wherever the owner's sense of place feels just right.

Many cabin dwellers seem to be shifting their activities and interests away from the more traditional fishing and hunting oriented vacations to more non-consumptive activities such as canoeing, birding, hiking, painting . . . even yoga, a great stress reliever. We often paddle down to a little resort store a mile or so from the cabin for ice cream or other essentials. We pass a dock where occasionally there is a couple sitting motionless in the lotus position, facing east, meditating and seemingly frozen in time. When we return an hour or so later, they are still there, still immobile. They never speak or acknowledge our passing. Like everyone else, they are doing their thing up at the cabin.

"Good Morning lake, Good Morning rocks, Good Morning trees, Good Morning Grandfather Raven!"

This is my regular early morning salutation as I step outside to greet my cabin world deep in the boreal forest on the south shore of Gunflint Lake along the Minnesota/Ontario Boundary Waters. Sometimes neighbors peer at me with a certain concern if they happen to be walking along the upper road or trolling past the dock doing their morning fishing therapy. I enjoy these communions and could never find similar relationships in a city. There isn't the beauty, the silence or the reverence there is at the early morning cabin, a venue that speaks to freedom, sanctuary and reflection. After many years of cabin-living in such close proximity, these rocks, trees and critters have become my friends, dignified, intimate and constant. I believe they have souls and that we connect regularly. The huge, striated chunks of glacier-carried granite have stories to tell of their travels and I feel the excitement as I lean into their shadows. I mourn when the big, 80-year-old white spruce tree down by the dock comes crashing down in a windstorm, but it has lived its life and I rejoice when I discover its offspring poking their fuzzy little green candles up through the carpet of brown needles on the forest floor. And Grandfather Raven, his splayed wing feathers scraping the wind, veers sharply out over the lake crawnking his displeasure at the quality and quantity of leftovers on his feeder.

Our little cabin neighborhood is an eclectic mixture of many lifestyles and agendas . . . about 100 people cabining on Gunflint Lake 50 miles from town on the edge of the wilderness. Occupancy can be from occasional weekends to two-week vacations or summer occupancy to year-round residence.

One of the most striking features about the lifestyle of this remote cabin community is how the people learn and share the fundamental tasks and skills of daily living with little professional help from the outside. We have a few neighbors who are generalists. They live here year-round and, of necessity, know how to do everything, but for most of us, survival is a learning experience, a work in progress. We don't bother calling the plumber because there are no plumbers, but how do you fix a toilet tank float? An electrical malfunction? A sinking fireplace? How do you build a room onto your cabin? What's the first thing you do? Almost none of my neighbors have any of these skills when they move in, but with diligence, energy and the help of the generalists they eventually acquire them. They are active or retired business people, physicians, engineers, contractors, salespersons, farmers, military personnel, accountants, teachers, lawyers, counselors, surveyors, clergy and artists, all of whom rely on the skills of the neighbors who probably learned just last year from another neighbor or one of the generalists to explain the mysteries of the plumbing, how to hook up an outdoor light fixture or how to level the dock.

In terms of workskills, especially carpentry, stone masonry, plumbing, electrical and motor repair, it is often a barter society. "If you fix my waterpump, I'll help install your cupboards," would be a common offering.

The answer to most simple repair or building problems is "do it yourself." One day I was admiring the way my neighbor Orv Gilmore, a retired college teacher, had re-structured his plumbing system to accommodate new needs.

"How in the world did you ever learn to do that?" I asked.

"I got a book in the library," was his response.

I am always amazed at the way several of these neighbors have acquired skills either from reading a book, watching another neighbor or just trying something, failing and trying again until it works. That seems to be the operative method. If you don't know how to do it, do it anyway. Then figure out what you did wrong and do it again.

Another rule is, "Never throw anything away." Someday one of the neighbors will need it. Greg Gecas, an owner of Heston's Lodge down the county road, is the ultimate practitioner of this rule. If any of us ever need a 1920 left-handed Dickerson-threaded plug, we would just ask Greg. He'll rummage around in one of his many treasure chests full of things he has kept because they may come in handy some day, hand it over and say, "Here, try this." Greg is a very key person in a neighborhood like this where the nearest big-box retailer is 150 miles away and the nearest hardware store is 50 miles way. We don't just run to the store when we need something. We see Greg first, and then do it ourselves.

This dependence on neighbors to provide fundamental help for living in a remote neighborhood is one of the aspects of community that is largely missing from most city neighborhoods. Add to that the vastness and the beauty of the natural environment here that makes our little enclave much more positive and friendly than any cityscape.

Cabin Journal Note:—

Good neighbors for many years, the late Fred and Lois Mauck lived in the oldest cabin on the lake. 1924 was the date carved into the lintel log above the front door. In their later years they could no longer split and carry the seven cords of wood needed to keep the cabin warm during the winter. One October morning six of the neighborhood men gathered up on the county road near the cabin where two dump trucks of 8-foot birch pulp stick logs had been delivered. Check Tiffany brought his log splitter and others brought axes, mauls, chain saws, wedges, ropes and all the equipment necessary for a wood-cutting party.

Lois supplied an endless flow of coffee and doughnuts and by 3 p.m. all seven cords were split and neatly stacked near the back door. Lois gave each of us hugs of gratitude and Fred gave each crew member a fake thousand dollar bill.

Chapter 2

A Place Like This

Technically, this part of the Superior National Forest is the sub-boreal forest, a mosaic of several forest communities, both coniferous and deciduous, south of the true boreal forest of the Canadian north. Its most outstanding features are the hundreds of lakes, rugged cliffs and occasional giant red and white pines, the trees which built America. They escaped the logging harvest of most pines here in the early century, due to being either inaccessible, diseased or on private property. The last of the big pines cut in this area were rafted down the Pigeon River in 1918. Some of these venerable trees which are left standing are nearly 150 feet tall now and were saplings when the Declaration of Independence was signed.

The northern part of this Gunflint region, about half land and half water, has an intriguing geomorphic history. The landscape is largely the result of ancient volcanic activity, glacial scouring and raging rivers moving over a variety of underlying bedrock structures. About 1.1 billion years ago, due to some big raisins in the dough of the molten earth called the Logan intrusives, these plugs were tilted up into the Rove Slate formations that shaped the present "sawtooth" topography. The region has nearly vertical cliffs which rise as high as 400 feet-forming what ecologist John Tester calls "the most rugged relief in the BWCA." These heavily forested headlands give the lakes a dimension and background that contribute a dramatic quality to their beauty.

Gunflint Lake dominates our little world as the lake does in most cabin venues. Gunflint is an eight-mile-long gash of glacial erosion in the Rove Slate and Gunflint iron with a maximum depth of over 200 feet, but it is more of a presence or personality than a geographical feature. It is beautiful, sometimes tempestuous, sometimes serene, inviting, ominous and always, it is the reason why we are here.

It saw the first wanderings of the Paleoindians as they hunted along the edge of the retreating glacier 10,000 years ago, Indians of the Archaic culture, the first Woodland Indian peoples and then early Cree and Ojibwe tribes. It saw the voyageurs of the fur trade century and the loggers of the Manifest Destiny period. Now it is the destination of vacationers, retirees, canoeists, sportsmen and a few permanent residents. Minnesota has more than 12,000 lakes over ten acres, most of which have family cabins on them, but for the cabin owner there is only one.

For me, the wild places and the wild things are the magic part of being at the cabin. The wildlife indigenous to any cabin area is surely one of the most looked for and cared for attractions. They are, after all, our closest neighbors at the cabin and were here long before we were.

In this part of the state, the black bear is a close and visible neighbor. We see the bears first in the spring when they come out of hibernation, gaunt, rail thin with dull, scraggly coats hopping carefully from moss to grass to leaf piles. The skin on their feet, normally callused and tough, is very tender and sore, as last year's hard leathery skin has sloughed off during hibernation and is replaced by a new sensitive cuticle. It will take a couple weeks for the skin on their feet to toughen enough to be comfortable when the bear jumps around on rocks and logs. Many of the females will have cubs with them in spring and when mom gives the warning woof, the cubs scamper up the nearest tree like squirrels.

The black bear, even though usually an amiable critter, is still a wild animal, so it is best to always be aware of its presence. We have a Bear Hot Line that keeps all the neighbors aware of the location of the latest bear sighting in the neighborhood. Neighbor Evelyn Wick usually activates the line. She is probably in the kitchen when she spots the bears out in the back yard and immediately telephones Carol Byer next door, who takes the message and passes it on to Les and Liz Edinger next door to her. "There's a good-sized bear out here in our yard," she informs them. "It is a female with one first-year cub and they're headed toward your driveway."

In a few moments our phone will ring and it will be Liz telling us about the bear and her cub ambling down the game trail toward our cabin. Out will come the field glasses for a close look and then, as they leave, we'll call the next cabin and so on down the lake as long as the bear stays near shore, which usually isn't very long. The bears often make short little trips out into the cabin neighborhoods just to see if any goodies have been left out by mistake, but then they soon retreat into their deeper woodland haunts.

Many of the cabins and woodsheds in this area have long claw marks on them where bears have tried to get at a bird feeder, the stored sacks of sunflower seeds and corn or a bee's honey cache under the eaves, but generally black bears are among the most tractable of neighbors. The residents, of course, would never provoke them or get between a mother and her cubs. We leave each other alone and get along fine. Unfortunately some resorts shoot them because they frighten their guests.

In spite of a sharp and unexplained population decrease, there are still several thousand moose in this Arrowhead region and they are seen frequently along the roads, especially in winter when they move along the shoulders on their front knees licking up the salt highway crews scatter, but we are still thrilled every time we spot one of these gentle giants in the yard or along a forest road.

We have a soft spot for these moose because they played a role in our cabin introduction. We began this project in 1980 when Frank Shunn, a crusty neighbor from Lake Saganaga, agreed to take on the task of remodeling and finishing the shabby shell of a cabin we had found. He was very creative and precise, a craftsman-type of the old cabin-builder school. We spent some time looking at several cabins he had built and were very impressed, but we couldn't start until Frank approved of us.

In those days we were both working in the Twin Cities area and when Julie could leave her teaching job at about 4 o'clock on Friday afternoon we would head for the lake and a weekend's work on the cabin helping Frank. That may be a little misleading. Frank would allow us to carry lumber, open nail boxes, tack up insulation bats, sweep up shavings and try to complete other critical tasks without getting in his way.

After a dinner stop along the way we would usually get to the cabin near midnight. One of the first times we came up was a moonless Friday night, and the trip up the Gunflint Trail was kind of a spooky ride for a couple of city folks. Our cabin site was about three miles off the Trail on a county road and our rough driveway turned off it through a 600-foot cedar grove on a sharp grade down to the lake.

We made the turn into the driveway and as the headlights probed the dark alley of cedars down to the lake, Julie yelped, "Yikes, what's that?"

At the bottom of the drive we saw four glowing, greenish orbs moving around near the lakeshore and came to a sudden stop. We were sure they belonged to some kind of animals but what kind? They were big eyes, quite high off the ground and moving back and forth slowly. What to do? We thought they were harmless, but we didn't know, and besides it was pitch black out, except for the headlights and those scary eyes moving around down there at the foot of the driveway. When you are a stranger to the forest wilderness and it is very dark, imaginations seem to run amok and I could envision two great, shaggy bears standing there swaying back and forth on their hind legs with slavering jaws just waiting for us to invade their space. It is rather humiliating to recall now, but we backed out of there, raced back down the county road to the Gunflint Trail and pulled into an overlook where we slept in the car all night. In the morning we went back, rolled down the driveway, got out of the car and found two sets of tracks around the cabin. One large set and one small set. Moose! A cow and her calf had been strolling around down there, and we like to think now, they were more of a welcoming committee than a threat.

We have some other ghostly megafauna around here but we seldom ever see them. The Eastern gray, or timber wolf, that animal naturalist/author Sparky Stensaas calls the most family-oriented animal in North America, travels in packs and probably numbers around 1800 here in northeastern Minnesota. They are very wary and seldom appear in public, although their tracks and scat are often seen on trails. We have only seen about a dozen wolves in 25 years and that is probably a pretty good average. Some reported sightings are probably coyotes, sometimes called brush wolves, or German Shepherd dogs. Carol Byer, the Gunflint Berry Lady, whose cabin is a couple doors down from us, had a very interesting and unusual experience with a wolf recently. She had a few motion-sensitive lights installed around her cabin. One night the "front yard" was suddenly a blaze of light, and when Carol got up to investigate, there was a full grown, grizzled, timber wolf looking in her living room window. They stared at each other for a minute or so and the wolf finally shrugged and melted back into the night shadows without seeming to move a muscle, as wolves often do. Carol said it looked rather gaunt so it was probably looking for something to eat.

The cougar, or mountain lion, has been seen by several people in this neighborhood, and that brings up a little problem. In order for any sighting to be recognized officially, the sighting report should be accompanied by a photograph, scat sample, exact location and if possible, a plaster cast of the track. These are not always required or possible to acquire, but are the surest way to credentialization. So most cougar sightings here are usually accompanied only by "Jeez, did you see that!" and that's the end of it except for the stories back in the neighborhood the next day.

When Donna Preus opened up her cabin last spring, she discovered the messy remains of a deer under the front porch. There was no reported sighting, but a wildlife biologist suggested it might have been a cougar kill, because the timber wolf usually devours his deer at the kill site, while the cougar often carries it off to eat more leisurely in a concealed place.

Cindy Tiffany, a neighbor who lives down the private road a couple miles away, had the most unusual cougar sighting in the neighborhood. She was returning home, driving down the narrow, gravel road, late one April night when suddenly, as she came over a hill, she saw three cougar rumps and swishing tails in the headlights. They were headed in the same direction she was at about the same speed. One veered left across the road and headed for the woods, giving Cindy a full broadside view of the big cat, and the others followed quickly. She was so enthralled by their presence, she stopped the car, got out and looked around, but when she became aware of the many night noises always present in the deep woods, she jumped right back in the car. She returned next morning to photograph the many tracks in the frozen mud which a DNR wildlife biologist later identified as the tracks of adult cougars.

Cindy is quite certain the cats came from the Canadian side of the still-frozen Gunflint Lake, which is only about a mile wide at that point. That area of Ontario is a total wilderness with only two east/west surfaced roads between the lake and the North Pole, while the American side is not as cougar-friendly with numerous cabins and resorts.

We even have a new wild neighbor more visible since the big storm in '99, the Canada Lynx, which isn't really new here, but the beautiful, dappled cat is recovering nicely from a serious population decline of many years. For a century the lynx was a desirable pelt sought by Minnesota trappers with thousands trapped in the state each year until the state ended lynx trapping in 1984, and they are now making a good comeback. They have a large range, sometimes as much as 300 miles. Many of them have been radio-collared and have been traced far north into Ontario, but they have come back to the Gunflint region and don't seem to be as shy as the wolves or deer. They are sometimes seen ambling along the Trail, holding their tufted ears and black-tipped tails high and seeming to enjoy the photo op they are providing visitors.

The neighbors down on the point, Bill and Mary Hatfield, have a very unique cabin site on a narrow point of land that defines the west end of Dog Ear Bay, a favorite sanctuary for nesting loons, feeding moose and playful otters. Bald eagles and ospreys patrol the skies above the 200-foot South Rim Trail ridge that looms over the bay. Deer seldom wander out onto the point because, always wary of the predator timber wolf, deer keep escape routes in mind and a point of land is a trap they avoid.

Because of the varied habitat of wetland, big timber, water and a heavy understory, the cabin site is literally a wildlife crossroad, and much of Bill's and Mary's time is spent watching their many wild neighbors. Much attention was given recently to a pair of daily moose visitors they named Lily, and her calf, Junior. They would show up for breakfast at sunrise every morning in July and August, pulling up lily pad plants and eating the roots, and then would come ashore next to the dock.

Junior was still small enough to walk under Lily's belly then, and they would come out of the water near the dock, stroll around the yard and then duck under the second-floor deck where Lily would lean up against the cabin and moan and groan as though she was in terrible pain. There didn't seem to be anything wrong with her, and Bill and Mary, seated on the deck above Lily, decided that maybe she was singing to them. This went on every day for two months during the summer and then one day the moose didn't show up and haven't been seen since.

One of the puzzles they have not been able to figure out is the antics of two otters who occasionally goose loons resting on the bay. The loons seem to think the bay is theirs alone and will sometimes rush and scream at any creature bold enough to venture onto its surface. Loons have a spotless image, but are not the harmless creatures everyone seems to think. They see other diving waterfowl as competition for food, and a favorite strategy is to drown the young of any other waterfowl, especially mergansers, by swimming underneath them, grabbing their feet and dragging them under. But they occasionally get their comeuppance from the otters who swim underneath the loons, cold nose them, then turn and dive while the loons leap several feet into the air emitting very un-loon-like squawks.

Then there is Le Roy, a herring gull, who accompanies Bill whenever he goes out fishing, keeps all the other gulls away with his squalling, gobbles up any leftover baitfish and cleans up after Bill guts out his catch. A shiny, dark brown pine marten, who has learned to open the kitchen door, often undulates in and waits for a handout from Mary.

Last year Bill and Mary had guests from the city who brought their nine-year-old daughter. She was fascinated by the wildlife around the cabin, especially a bald eagle who came almost every day and sat on the top branch of a giant, old white spruce near the end of the point. Sometimes the eagle would spread his wings, push off the branch and then fold his wings, tip forward and plummet down to snatch a fish from near the surface of the bay, flying back to the treetop to enjoy his lunch at leisure. The little girl was fascinated by this great bird with its pure white head and tail, the powerful golden saber of a beak and its regal bearing. What gripped her was not so much the bird's presence or its appearance, but the fact that there really was such a thing as an eagle in the wild. She had never been here before, nor ever seen an eagle. She had seen pictures and many representations of eagles, but her sense of wonder was ignited by having this real live eagle in the tree above her. She was mesmerized. Eagles will do that to you.

The birds are always the first critters up in the morning here. Loons, crows and whitethroats are usually the ones we hear just as a ribbon of light is prying the night's lid off the eastern sky. As the day progresses there will be a parade of black-capped chickadees, chipping sparrows, jays (blue and gray), rose-breasted grosbeaks, red-breasted nuthatches and ruby-throated hummingbirds in the trees and at the feeder. Often a huge raven swoops in low to check out the possibilities of the feeder containing something a little more substantial than sunflower seeds, and a comical white herring gull comes tromping across the cabin roof like Charlie Chaplin on his huge flat feet, peering over the edge to see what is available.

My favorite visitor is a merlin, a small hawk, who speeds through the nearby forest hunting small birds and has its big nest of sticks about 100 feet up in a towering old white pine near the east end of the property. The merlin pair has come every spring to nest and raise their family here, seldom successfully, because a squadron of crows yells at them all day long, sometimes driving them off to an alternate nest in a huge old aspen tree on the Warren Road across the lake.

The merlin is a "small dashing falcon," according to the Peterson Field Guide. When perched, it appears to be a rather nondescript overall dark gray little hawk, but in flight overhead it flashes almost vivid underwings, breast and leg feathers which are sharply barred in brown and white. The dark brown tail has three distinct gray and white bands. Merlins fly in a straight line, seldom soar and never hover. I have never seen them do it, but the Peterson Guide says the merlin arrows directly into a group of flying birds at great speed, and snatches the slowest one out of the air. In full flight it screams and near the nest or perched on the top branch of a nearby tree, it whistles loudly.

We have other raptors around here: many owls, bald eagles, broadwing hawks, ospreys, red-tailed hawks, little sharpshins and Cooper's hawks. The merlins, however, are part of our cabin scene. They return each year to the big pine on our property. This makes them special.

Strictly speaking, the flowers of the ground-covering Canadian carpet are part of the wildlife here at the cabin. White violet, star flower, bunchberry, strawberry, Canada mayflower, nodding trillium, the tiny pinkish white blossoms of the twisted stalk and the three spikey balls of the wild sarsaparilla are among the first to appear in the spring. Many of these are white, shade-intolerant flowers and appear on the forest floor before the trees and shrubs foliate. Some white fruit tree and shrub blossoms also appear early. Pin cherry, thimbleberry and raspberry are among the first. In the open, sunny places, the heavenly blue forget-me-nots are out early, even before the bunchberry blossoms. Next to appear are the yellow flowers: clintonia, tall buttercup, wild mustard, St. John's Wort, cinquefoil and yellow hawkweed along the road. This is also the time when the leaves begin to come out and there is a touch of color beginning in the woods and along the game trails as the shade-tolerant moccasin flowers, Virginia bluebells and calypso orchids add their flashes of lavender and pink to the woodland scene.

Cabin Journal Note:—
Pip was born and raised over in the Round Lake country a few miles west of the Gunflint Trail. I knew her family but our period of residence didn't mesh, I have always considered Pip a neighbor even though she married and moved

away from here years ago. Her real name was Roberta and she owned a chocolate shop in Minnetonka, but she was Pip to every one here and she visited often, staying with her sister Debbie Mark, owner of Seagull Outfitters.

In 1998 she was diagnosed with a virulent, often terminal cancer, and moved back here to the country she loved so deeply. Debbie cared for her and flew her all over the country to various clinics and cancer centers hoping to find a cure, but nothing seemed to help for long.

When she died, about 50 friends and neighbors gathered at the old canoe landing on the Cross River where it makes a wide, slack water curve before it narrows into a chute of granite chunks. From there, it begins its riffley journey through the pines and between the hills to its outflow under the bridge at the west end of Gunflint Lake.

Pip's ashes were deposited into an upstream stretch of the Cross and as they came past the canoe landing on her final river run, her friends made their silent tributes and farewells to her memory, each in their own way, as Pip's sense of place found expression in her choice for final rest. It was the most appropriate and moving memorial service I have ever attended.

Chapter 3

SKETCHES FROM THE NEIGHBORHOOD

SOME CABINS ARE BUILT IN REMOTE AREAS with pure solitude and escape as a goal, but most are part of a neighborhood, whatever its size may be. The factors that unite are the environment, friendship and the owner's desire to be part of a small community of like-minded folks. Also, should the need arise for help of any kind (always a problem in a remote area), it is always nearby.

Much can be told about the nature and interests of a cabin neighborhood by scanning its Internet bulletin board. A look at borealnews. org each morning tells much about the concerns, interests and goings-on of this neighborhood.

On a recent morning a woman wrote of finding a dead cow moose in her cabin yard and a calf wandering around in the nearby woods. She wondered if a moose calf that size could survive on available vegetation and if not, what should she do? The DNR responded quickly, sending a crew out to take blood samples from the dead moose to see if a cause of death could be determined, and also to attempt to locate the calf. These men on the DNR crew are not veterinary medical examiners, so a precise cause of death couldn't be pinpointed, but they did determine that she was fairly old, had several calves over the years and was in a low-feed area, so they ascribed her death to natural causes. At last report they hadn't caught the calf, but they did chase it around the woods for a while, and it always stayed ahead of them. It appeared strong and there was some browse there for it to eat, so they didn't see any reason to continue the chase. They were quite certain it would survive. The following sketches may further clarify the unique character of this cabin neighborhood.

Baking and Breaking Bread Together

A memory of disappearing Americana occurs weekly in the summer and fall here in this cabin neighborhood, which I feel is probably one of the few venues left in our society where community bread-baking occurs. This is a neighborhood event, or ritual, in which the baking is done in an outdoor wood-fired, retained-heat oven which Greg built with the help of Allen Scott who is with Ovencrafters of Petaluma, California, and who was here to teach the course in oven building at the North House Folk School in Grand Marais. The school offers a three-day course in the construction, firing and use of these ovens whose American history goes back to colonial times.

This is an impressive structure. Made of brick and stone it is a square 6 by 6 feet, 10 feet high and with an oven that is 32 by 36 inches. It is set in a grove of old cedar trees which overhang a picnic table that is more of a 12-foot bread board, all in back of the lodge where the neighbors gather weekly in an ice cream social atmosphere. In some respects, the event resembles a quilting bee or a barn raising, in that the neighbors get together to collectively accomplish something as fundamental as bread baking in a spirit of community. It provides an opportunity for neighbors to visit, exchange recipes and sample each other's bread, pastry or pizza crust. The oven is big enough to bake 15 loaves at a time in 17 minutes, and there are always willing hands enough to bake a week's supply of bread for many families, and to do so in a congenial party atmosphere.

On a sparkling September morning neighbors and guests drifted down to the grove in the back yard of Heston's Lodge. The oven was to be ready at 10 a.m.

There was much discussion about the baking process, bread types and the interior condition of the oven. Preparation for baking starts the day before when a fire is built in the oven and the interior is allowed to soak up the heat overnight. In the morning, the ashes are cleared out and a bigger, hotter fire is built. This time the goal is to bring the interior temperature up to 550 degrees. At this point Barb Gecas gives it the Flour Test. She sprinkles a handful of flour in the hot oven. If it burns up immediately and disappears the oven is too hot. If it lasts for about ten seconds, before charring, the oven is ready. It is then cleaned out, and the door closed tightly until the bread is put in. Just before the loaves are put into the oven, Barb spritzes a cloud of water mist from a spray bottle into the oven. This raises the humidity and promises a good crust. The bread, of course, was mixed at the cabin in each baker's kitchen and each one brings the raised dough in a bowl, on a cookie sheet or in bread pans, ready for the oven. Greg has made a long-handled paddle out of blowdown birch which is coated with corn-meal to allow the bread to slide easily and then used to insert the bread in the oven.

On this particular morning there were about 20 of us gathered at the big table Greg built out of 12-foot storm-downed birch planks and which are kept scrubbed so the bread dough can be rolled and loaves cut right on the table at ovenside.

Barb had brought a couple loaves of desam, a Flem-ish no-yeast, whole wheat bread, and Sharlene Le Tourneau had her sourdough ciabatta loaves which only bake from 5 to 8 minutes in that extreme heat. The word "ciabatta" is Italian for slipper, and that is a pretty good description of the loaf's shape. This is particularly inter-esting bread because Sharlene has had the starter for 16 years and brings it down from Alaska every year for this neighborhood bread baking get-together. It is an "herby" bread with pinches of oregano, basil and a little garlic. During our taste test we tear off a hunk and dip it in pasta sauce or warm olive oil.

Barb told me that one woman had baked a batch of dog biscuits even though she didn't have a dog, but thought the neighbor's dog would like them. Jody Preus and Bonnie Morris had pans of whole grain yeast bread and Fred Smith brought his locally famous sesame butter-milk bread which suffered an inglorious fate on this par-ticular day. He was going to gild the lily by brushing an egg wash on the crust, which was incinerated in the 550-degree oven. Fred retrieved the blackened loaves and broke one open. The bread inside was delicious, but the crust was ruined.

We all know better than to slice and eat freshly baked bread, but many bakers bring an extra loaf for consumption at the party so we munch loudly and heap praise on the bakers while the kids clean up anything left on the table and Greg's chickens scurry around underneath the table cleaning up the crumbs. The place is spotless when we leave.

The Last Real Indian

Across the lake, on the Ontario side in a little bay near the abandoned railroad grade, lived a man who was, for me, the Last Real Indian. Charley Cook was mostly Ojibwe, and maybe part Cree. He spoke a patois containing words and phrases reminiscent of several different tribes. There were some words for everyone. Very few, not even his Ojibwe friends up at the Grand Portage Reservation, understood him perfectly, although almost everyone could understand enough to get his message. He was a man of great natural dignity with a presence which was understated but sensed immediately. He had a slim athletic build and a full head of jet black hair when he died at age 95. From the ceiling of Charley's cabin on the Canadian shore bay hung an array of dried wild plants, the natural, traditional medicines used by generations of Charley's family. He had a remedy for just about anything. Especially effective for colds was a tea made from the stringy inner bark of the aspen.

One night of bright moonlight when Justine Kerfoot, his longtime neighbor and friend, was canoeing along the Canadian shore on her way back to the lodge, she came upon Charley chanting and dancing on a flat rock that jutted out into the lake. She assumed he was involved in a ritual of his religion and slipped past without a greeting, but, out of curiosity, later returned to the exposed reef along shore, hoping to find a pictograph or some evidence of a holy place, but it remained moss-covered and undisturbed. Charley's spiritual and physical life were strongly bound to ancient codes and symbols.

Most of these things he kept to himself and never spoke of them to his white neighbors, but some of his actions clearly showed cultural influences.

The black bear was, according to Ojibwe scholar Basil Johnson in his book *Ojibwe Heritage*, a totemic figure, revered for his physical strength and courage. It is said that the old Ojibwe would not kill a bear and would not guide parties of white hunters whose goal was to kill a bear. Some of Charley's activities in his later years were perhaps echoes of old Ojibwe messages he had heard.

A bear story about Charley which has circulated around the neighborhood for years tells of him finding an orphaned cub in the woods one spring and taking it home to his cabin to feed. The cub got to hanging around the cabin whenever he got hungry and as the seasons turned Charley realized that without a mother to gather him into the hibernation den the poor little guy might freeze during the coming winter. So he arranged a cozy little place under his own bed in the cabin and took the little bear in for the winter. Come spring the little bear scampered off into the woods and never came back to Charley's.

When Charley was well into his 90s, some of his friends decided that it would be better if he would move into the senior apartment facility in town. They didn't think he should be living in an isolated cabin in the woods at his age. Charley went along with the idea and seemed to enjoy his new surroundings. But one day the administration of the care unit decided they would have to discipline him because he was saving food scraps and throwing them out his second-story back window for the bears who visited regularly, as the apartment unit was right on the woodsy edge of town. It seems that some of the other residents became frightened of the bears wandering around in back of the home and complained loudly.

Canoe Racing to the Rescue

The annual canoe races are the social event of the Gunflint season. In 27 years they have gone from a neighborhood fund raiser to help finance a much-needed rescue squad and volunteer fire department to a well publicized event that brings hundreds of people to Gunflint Lodge waterfront every July, and thousands of dollars to the Gunflint Trail Volunteer Fire Department for equipment and training. Anyone can register to participate but the racers are mainly vacationers, summer residents and resort or outfitter staffs. With the exception of the long distance race that kicks off the event, the racing is more entertainment than serious sport. Speed sprints, broken paddles, mixed ages and facing racers are featured, but the last race usually draws the most attention. It is a gunn'l pumping event where the racers stand balanced on the rear gunn'ls and "pump" with their legs bouncing the bow of the canoe up and down and sending it, hopefully forward, in a somewhat straight line. It is a sport for young strong legs and usually results in over half the racers scrambling around in the water for overturned canoes. This every-summer get together features rides in the big Voyageur canoes brought down from the Plymouth Youth Center wilderness canoe base on Seagull Lake, aqua-golf, which is chipping floating golf balls into an anchored canoe and minnow races for the little kids.

Huge amounts of food and baked goods are prepared in cabins around Gunflint, Seagull and Saganaga Lakes, whose owners join the Gunflint folks in sponsoring the races. A feature of the event is a silent auction of beautifully crafted items such as castle-like bird feeders and intricate Norwegian knitwear which the makers work on for months before the auction evening. Long tables full of art work, canoeing equipment, dinner-for-two certificates and items from local merchants are distributed in an evening-long raffle of which the top prize is a new 17-foot canoe donated by the manufacturer. The whole glorious evening attracts several hundred people from all over the area who provide the Gunflint Trail Volunteer Fire Department, which has included the Rescue Squad since March of 2000, with several thousand dollars for equipment and training. This is another example of neighbors pooling their resources, creativity and energies to do a job that badly needed doing.

For many years there was no emergency medical service or fire-fighting capability on the Gunflint Trail. In 1950 residents relied on the services available in Grand Marais, 50 miles away, where there was one doctor, one nurse and a local pastor with an old station wagon that passed for an ambulance. The Wilderness Act of 1964 brought thousands of canoeists into the Boundary Waters

Canoe Area with the major eastern area access on Lake Saganaga at the end of the Gunflint Trail. Soon the Sag Landing was the goal of many rescue boats bringing in victims of campfire burns, axe cuts, broken bones from falls on portages, heart attacks and all manner of medical emergencies, but there was no emergency medical service or ambulance to transport them the last 55 miles to the hospital except by residents' cars and volunteers' pickup trucks. In addition to local medical needs this situation on the Gunflint Trail became critical.

In the mid-1970s four Gunflint area residents took an advanced first aid course taught by a local nurse. They were encouraged to start a rescue squad which would serve the Gunflint Trail, as the population north of town was growing rapidly. Letters were sent out to residents and business owners in the region, who responded generously and the Gunflint Trail Rescue Squad was started. That first group was small and couldn't offer much more than caring attention, first aid and a rickety old ambulance they bought from Silver Bay for one dollar. In March of 2000 the Rescue Squad was merged with the Gunflint Trail Volunteer Fire Department. Members took many hours of emergency medical training in Duluth at their own expense. Two local property owners donated land and a new building to house equipment. Still small, but it was a good start, and with several grants of near $1 million, fundraisers, local help and the annual Gunflint Trail Canoe Races, they have grown over the years into one of the most highly trained and well equipped rural volunteer fire departments and rescue squads in the state.

The Hoover Cabin Next Door

The author Helen Hoover and her illustrator husband Ade used to live in a small cabin without water, heat or electricity next door from 1949 until they left in 1970 to settle in Taos, New Mexico. Helen often became nostalgic about the Gunflint cabin. She once came back for a visit and later wrote:

"I knew at that moment that this was still, and always will be our place . . . [The cabin] is where you find the fulfillment of your deepest needs, and you find it only once if you are lucky enough to find it at all. But, once you find it, you never leave it entirely, and you never lose it, because it has become a part of you."

Helen knew about cabins.

Behind our woodshed, and through a small remnant of old growth birch, spruce, cedar and a few towering white pines, sits the small Kentucky-style log cabin with its signature twin gables, probably the only one of that unique design in this part of the country. Also in the reclaiming forest are the ice house Ade used as a studio, Helen's writing cabin and the forlorn little tarpaper hen house of Bedelia and the Crown Prince, a chicken and a rooster that provided eggs and amusement.

The cabin was built in the '30s by Walt Yocum, a trapper and logger, who had come up here looking for a little more space and freedom than he found in his native Kentucky. It was bought in 1949 by the Hoovers as they left their jobs in Chicago for a new life in the wilds of Gunflint country along the Ontario border. Helen is best known for her four nature books: *The Long Shadowed Forest* in 1963; *Gift of the Deer* in 1966 (a Reader's

Digest Condensed Book); *A Place in the Woods*, 1969; and *Years of the Forest*, a cabin reminiscence written in Taos, New Mexico in 1973. Not as well known are her children's books, *Animals at My Doorstep*, *Great Wolf and the Good Woodsman* and *Animals Near and Far*. Even less well known are her adult romances, written under the pseudonym of Jennifer Price, which she wrote for subsistence money during the lean years before she became rich and famous for her nature books.

Helen was a feisty lady and didn't get along too well with some of the neighbors. She would be called a brusque and outspoken environmental activist today and would perhaps find much empathy here now, but the word "environmentalist" or its meaning were not in common use until Rachel Carson wrote *Silent Spring* in 1962. Helen was many years before her time in her concern for environmental issues.

From next door a definite mood or ambience still lingers, especially on moonlit winter nights when the deer gather in the clearing. Reading Helen's books several times and re-living their experiences here many years before we arrived has given us an insight into their apprehensions and a respect for their convictions as bulldozers and chain-saws shattered their dreams and hunters shot the deer on their property as they came into the clearing to feed.

Other than the buildings which the current owners have retained, the only reminder of the Hoover's residence here is the occasional elderly pilgrim wandering down the neighbor's driveway asking, "Is this the Helen Hoover cabin?" Twenty-five or thirty years ago it was common for people to stop up on the road and come down to see the place. They were very knowledgeable, had read all the Hoover books and were thrilled to be at her cabin. We got to calling them pilgrims because they seemed to be on a holy mission. These original Hoover fans are becoming less numerous. They are white-headed now and come down the drive with canes or walkers, but occasionally one will show up, still enthusiastic and starry-eyed.

The Otters

It is almost an automatic reaction, or a nervous tic. Most cabin dwellers automatically glance out at the lake hundreds of times a day. Nobody is really looking for anything. It's just something everyone does. Look out at the lake. Whose canoe is that going past? Is that a fish that jumped out near the big rock? Is the wind changing? What's going on out on the lake?

My wife Julie and Melinda Johnson were on their way down to the dock with their lunch one August Sunday morning and did a quick double take. There were three otters peeking up over the edge of the dock, their slick wet heads glistening and each of them churring or chattering in that strange language of disturbed otters. The Northern river otters are sometimes called the "playboys of the animal world." Naturalist Sparky Stensaas calls them "boreal buffoons," and tells us they are the only truly amphibious members of the weasel family, about 4 feet long and weighing about 20 pounds. " It is a lustrous brown with a silvery wash on the muzzle and throat," he says.

They were there because the dock is a great fishing spot on sunny days. It is a 16-foot square floater made of planks and styrofoam logs which creates a large cool, shady shadow spot in the water where small fish crowd in and occasionally predators, like the otters, dart in to grab one.

The dogs were sniffing and running around in circles excitedly. There was splashing and yipping coming from under the dock. Julie discovered that an otter had gotten caught under the dock and was not only making a big fuss about it but was giving great concern to his friends hanging on the edge of the dock who now took off swimming across the lake in their smooth, undulating glide. What to do? It was a Sunday and no DNR personnel were available. Nobody could figure out how to free the otter so they hurried next door to see if Duncan and Ev McDonald had any ideas. Dunc brought a long pole over and tried poking around under the dock, but couldn't seem to dislodge the otter. Julie rang neighbors Ev and John Wick for their advice and they suggested calling Miranda Kerfoot, the manager down at the lodge, who said she'd be right there and bring their naturalist with her.

Now there were seven rescuers on the dock. They all got down on their hands and knees peering through the half-inch slots between dock boards and glimpsed whiskers and a bright eye. It was the otter, wedged between chunks of blue styrofoam flotation material. They had found the otter but they couldn't free it. The sounds of its struggle were getting fainter and more plaintive.

Pretty soon Ev's husband John, who had been watching the football game, came over with his chain saw and a pry bar. Now there were 8 people on the dock. It was suggested that they all get on one side and the other side, containing the trapped otter, would come up out of the water and maybe it could wiggle loose. The dockful of people crowded onto one side, lifted the other side clear of the water with the otter still trapped and wiggling. Good plan, but it didn't free the otter. Next, John cut a small hole near where they figured the otter was and Julie put an open can of tuna fish in the hole thinking the tuna fish might be enough of an incentive for the otter to free itself. That didn't work either. The otter was still stuck. John then lifted one of the16-foot dock planks up with his pry bar. Voila! The otter came up with it, still locked in his styrofoam prison. Willing hands pulled the blocks away and the otter was freed.

Everyone assumed the rescued otter would rejoin his friends on the Canadian side of the lake as quickly as it could, but for some reason it hung around until evening, but was gone the next morning.`

Cabin Journal Note:—
Many stories about northeastern Minnesota people will inevitably include the Ojibwe. But how do you spell that word? It also is seen in many publications as Ojibway, Ojibwa, or even Chippewa, the white man's interpretation of the tribal name. Chippewa is not culturally correct, but it is commonly used and became part of treaty language. It is used for both the people and their ancestral language in Michigan, Minnesota, North Dakota and Wisconsin. In the *Ojibwe Word Resource Book*, by Nichols and Nyholm, it says, "Ojibwe or Ojibwa is the name used in Ontario and Salteaux is used in Manitoba and Saskatchewan . . . it is difficult to draw sharp boundaries around these linguistic and social groups."

My resource person to whom I often turn in these matters is an elder of the Grand Portage Ojibwe band and he indicates it doesn't really make much difference how you spell it because it was not a written language for many years after their hegira here from their Algonquin homeland in the northeastern U.S.

Chapter 4

WATER AND WOOD—
THE ESSENTIALS

MOST OF US WHO LIVE ALONG THIS SHORE of Gunflint Lake use its water for drinking, cooking and washing. A rapidly disappearing gift of Nature from the icy depths, it is still pure and safe as long as it is properly filtered. Water from near the surface should never be used due to the potential presence of the giardia, an intestinal parasite which enters the water from the wastes of beavers and waterfowl. The County requires that submersible pumps be installed at a minimum of 18 feet below the surface to be safe from the pesky little giardia bugs. Neighbor Jerry Caple keeps track of its clarity with regular trips around the lake with his Secci Disc rig and reports to the country Soils and Water department clarity to 24 feet, or "just about what it was 300 years ago." I'm always glad to hear that but I am curious to know how they know what it was like 300 years ago.

Those few who don't use lake water have wells, but most hesitate to drill wells because no one ever seems to know at what depth water will be found. One neighbor drilled down close to 1,000 feet and didn't find enough water to open more than one faucet at a time, and still others find adequate water at less than 100 feet. There doesn't seem to be a very accurate way of predetermining at what depth water in sufficient quantity and quality will be found. Another problem with drilling a well is that you may get salt water. Back many millions of years ago this was a shallow tropical sea and there are still pockets of salt water down there. Some of the nearby state parks have both fresh and salt water taps.

It is difficult to believe that science and engineering can't do everything better than it used to be done, but we never seemed to have this problem before when Bob Nelson, the Water Witch, was alive. Bob and his wife Greta were a delightful Swedish couple who came to Gunflint via Chicago where Bob was a master carpenter and cabinetmaker. They had been looking around the north country for a cabin site when they heard about a piece of property for sale on Gunflint Lake. They drove up to see it one August day in 1941 and were having a picnic on the lot beneath a big pine tree near shore when a fawn in a red sweater came out of the woods and stood looking at them. That did it. They decided immediately this was the place for them. The fawn in the red sweater was a neighborhood pet which Charley Olson, the caretaker of many summer residences, had rescued from an ice floe the previous spring during ice out and for which Justine had knit a sweater to make it visible to deer hunters. Justine wanted to keep the fawn in the ice house during the deer season to keep it safe but Charley didn't want the fawn locked up and thought the red sweater would protect it, but during the season a hunter shot it with a handgun.

Bob built their small jewel box of a cabin a little bit at a time, finishing a new section every summer vacation. It wasn't completely finished until about 1951 and when we came in 1979, they were our good neighbors for 10 years. One of the many ways Greta endeared herself to us was by making genuine Swedish egg coffee for 60 or 70 cabin residents for the annual neighborhood picnic at the east end beach opening the summer season.

Bob and Greta, who both learned dowsing in Sweden from family members, were infallible at finding "live" underground water, never rain runoff or contaminated water. They would march around a property in lock step, holding a forked, flexible willow stick, with hands held palms in with the two prongs between them, waiting for the single end, pointed straight ahead, to be pulled irresistibly downward. "Dig here," Bob would say, and that would inevitably be successful.

Dowsing, or water witching, as it is often called, has been traced through history, back to 2200 BC. Walker Wyman, an emeritus professor at the University of Wisconsin, wrote a book, *Witching For Water, Oil, Pipes and Precious Minerals*, in which he says that more than 225,000 wells were dowsed along the east coast of America in the Colonial century. Dowsing, which is usually done with a peeled, forked stick, either willow or birch, has been done with nylon rods, twigs, even coat hangars or saw blades. Many scientists and hydrologists call dowsing a hoax, but the well drillers have been calling in the dowsers for years when they come up with dry holes.

Next-door neighbor Orv, although he was very skeptical to begin with, found his water at 8 feet, near the corner of his cabin, after following Bob's instructions. No one knows how or why it worked, but it did and even though both Bob and Greta are gone now, the water they found in the neighborhood is still flowing.

Before my neighbor Les Edinger was my plumber he was an engineer for Honeywell, worked on the Space Shuttle and the team which built the navigation system that sent the first Boeing 757 around the world . . . and him with it. I figured he was qualified to handle the repair of my rinky-dink water system that sucked the water out of the lake and sent it through a pressure tank, a webwork of funny looking pipes under the cabin and into an ultra-violet filtering complex. When he came over with his power wagon full of tools, he was confident he could find the reason for some serious pressure problems producing weird noises in the pipes every time we turned a faucet on or flushed the toilet. He disappeared under the cabin into the "pump room," where he made all kinds of strange noises for an hour or so.

Finally, he came up and said, "I think I have found the problem but we need a few things. We will have to take a close look at the pressure switch to check the inter-face. Then we'll need an M1 and an M2, but that is another configuration. Then we can tie back into the pressure switch." Engineers sure talk funny. I learned long ago that when Les starts talking like that, my best response is to rub my chin thoughtfully and say, "Mmm, very interesting." I didn't have the foggiest notion of what he was talking about, but I followed his plumbing supply order instructions as best I could and it worked out fine. It was another excellent local example of how neighbors with skills help neighbors with no skills. The important thing is to balance the books with reciprocating help.

Wood is another important item in the development of a cabin neighborhood. In earlier days heat and shelter were two priorities that wood from the surrounding forest provided. Now heat in newer cabins comes from oil, propane, electricity or solar energy, but there are still many wood stoves and fireplaces which provide some heat and much of the cabin aesthetic.

This, of course, requires a supply of firewood, and strangely, it is at a premium here in the forest. There are primarily coniferous trees here and they are so full of resin that all of them are unsuitable for firewood. Burning any coniferous wood results in an accumulation of resin in the chimney, which eventually will burst into a flaming chimney fire. Standing dead jackpine or white spruce is usable primarily on cool mornings to "take the chill off," but not as a main heating source.

The next most numerous tree here is the aspen, or "popple," but it burns like rolled-up newspaper—hot and fast. There is some maple, a fine firewood, growing farther down toward the North Shore, but it has to be trucked up here, adding considerably to the cost. Birch is the most commonly used firewood here and it is pretty good, but the birch is dying off rapidly and it rots soon after it dies or is cut. Loggers say that birch starts rotting as soon as it is cut and falling, and is half rotten by the time it hits the ground. The rot produces soft, punky wood making it useless for firewood.

The woodshed is an auxiliary structure, like the outhouse, which makes the cabin a lifestyle rather than just a building. Most well-kept woodsheds have three different sizes of wood at hand in addition to a box of birch bark strips and pieces which are used for fire starter. When an eight- or ten- inch thick chunk is split in half, the two pieces can be kept for the woodpile. Wood bigger than that should be split again into fourths and then into eighths or smaller for the stove wood pile or the kindling bin. It all depends on the size of the chunk you start with. Kindling, the finely cut sticks of stove wood that get the fire going, is usually kept separately either in a box or in its own neat stack. Stovewood is one size up and is used in the woodstove or the heating fire between kindling and the big chunks which provide the longer burning heat for an all-day or night fire.

There is a saying in New England that a man can be judged by the condition of his woodshed. There is something deeply satisfying about filling a woodshed with even rows of hand-split wood. In *Shaped by Wind and Water*, Ann Zwinger's gardener observes. "You don't just stack wood, you place it." She continues this paragraph on placing wood by saying, "The ends of the fresh cut wood, a right angle joined by a curve, nestle against each other to form unexpected patterns of serpentines, spirals and swirls. The stacked wood is a handsome creation of its unconscious interplay of natural forms and colors . . . "

Splitting wood is not usually an on-purpose kind of a task, like painting the cabin, or re-roofing. It is more of a therapy activity, to be done occasionally rather than as one continuous job of work with a beginning and an end. One goes out to the woodshed to split wood when the stress level rises, when tight muscles need a little exercise, when the decibel level of grandchildren's music gets too high or a knotty problem needs some hard-thinking time. There is great healing in a half-hour of woodshed time. A little chipmunk I call Stubby helps to make my woodshed time pleasant. He has no tail. It was probably nipped off by a pine marten in a frantic chase. Chipmunks and red squirrels are the favorite food of pine martens around here, but we seem to have a stable population of all three. When I am stacking wood, Stubby sits on one of the chopping blocks and chatters at me, moving his head from side to side as though we are having a conversation. I guess maybe we are because I often answer him.

Most 10 by 12-foot woodsheds hold about six or seven cords of split wood, which is a winter's supply for a small, insulated cabin. After it is cut and split, most wood should dry for a year or so before it is burned, so most woodsheds are at least partially full and fragrant with the smell of freshly cut wood year-round.

My woodshed treasures have little monetary value but they are like gems to me. These are the sturdy, well used handmade tools, forged, shaped and carved of available materials and necessity, each for a specific task. They aren't worn out or broken, but scarred with years of heavy use and shiny with the patina of many craftsmen's hands and loving care.

These are the tools that cleared the land, split the firewood, built the cabins, boats and furniture, skinned the beavers and butchered the moose. The history of the land is hidden in these tools and as I heft them I am always aware of the hands that have guided them and the tasks they have performed. They have come to me in a

variety of ways; some were given to me, others were rescued from junk piles or were perhaps a lucky find at one
of those sad distributions of lives gone by called "estate
sales." Some were found scattered in the brush of deserted
lumber camps or on century-and-a-half-old cabin sites
where all the wooden, organic things rotted away but the
tempered steel of the double-bitted axehead was still
buried in the chopping block.

This hand-axe with the halberd blade, flat on one
side and sharply angled to a fine edge on the other, was
used to notch and fit cabin logs cleanly. The blade is hand
shaped and smithy formed. The double-bitted cruiser axe
hanging next to it was probably used to cut brush, limb
tree trunks, split firewood and do other camp chores. It
may even have been swung at a marauding bear. The
black ash handle has been rubbed to a shiny finish and the
blade edge still bears the grooves of a fine file. Sharpening
hand tools was a very precise ritual after every use in
those early days. After filing and stoning the blade, the
axeman would spit on the back of his hand and try to
shave the hair off with the sharpened blade. The axe was-
n't sharp enough until there was a bare spot on the back
of his hand.

This utility knife with the 12-inch blade was made
from a logging camp band saw blade which had probably
been discarded in the woods after many filings had worn
the teeth away. It has a moose antler handle, precisely cut
and fastened to the tang with dime-sized brass rivets. The
heavy blade is an eighth-inch wide at the top but is
tapered down to a scalpel edge. Heavy and sharp enough
to cut off a moose haunch or chop ice away from a beaver

set, but with it is a subtle, sweeping curve of the upper blade to the wide tip, ideal for skinning a big animal without puncturing the hide.

The drawshave, too, was cut from a lumber camp saw blade. Its handcarved wooden handles have bulbous ends that fit precisely into cupped hands. It was used for skinning logs, smoothing out knots, and in the hands of an expert logworker could produce a log that looked like it had been turned out on a lathe.

I found the heavy logging chain draped over a sagging gate near a deserted lumber camp. Each link is handmade from rod steel, the marks of the blacksmith's heavy hammer still plainly visible. The chain is rusty but serviceable and is still used to move logs around.

These are brawny, hard-working tools, but when used by a wood craftsman, they performed like an artist's brush. Most of these treasures just hang on the shed wall, but that is an appropriate place for them, because to me they are works of art and deserve gallery space.

Mary Colton, co-founder of the Museum of Northern Arizona, wrote about the handmade tools she gathered from the desert for the museum:

"These are the only ghosts I believe in, these eloquent personal things man has made with his hands . . . they are forever his and through the ages, breathe to us who pass, the spirit of their maker."

When a cabin is built or remodeled now, all the material is trucked up from the lumber yard in town, but it wasn't long ago that cabins and sheds were built from wood taken from the owner's property. The right amount of trees for a project was calculated, felled, limbed and hauled to the mill for ripping and planing into two by fours and whatever other sizes of lumber were needed. Knowing the characteristics of the various woods available was important to the builder. For example, balsam fir has good vertical strength so is useful for studdings, but as a horizontal member it is a real weakling.

Jackpine is a good building log, knotty but very strong. It's a good idea to let it sit for several months after cutting before it is worked. White cedar is an excellent building log and siding board, but available cedars are decreasing now because they have been cut for use in cabin building for a long time and, being very slow growing, they are not replacing themselves as building logs. Those cabins, which are now built of cedar logs or cedar siding, have the wood shipped in from the Pacific Northwest. Tamarack is best for docks and boat ramps because it is arrow straight, very strong and never rots even when wet. Most conifers here have a peculiar characteristic. If they are kept all dry or all wet, they will last a long time. If they are half wet and half dry, they will rot and weaken quickly. That is one reason for getting the bark off a cut log quickly. Moisture is held under the bark, so if the log is skinned as soon as the tree is cut, the wood will last for a long time.

Cabin Journal Note:—
Neighbor Chuck Lang, writing in his 2001 Fall Report of the Gunflint Supply Company, has this note on the difference between engineers and muddlers.

"Let me tell you, I happen to believe those who mud-dle through survive pretty well by trial and error methods and seem just as happy as engineers who have no appre-ciation for happenstance. They have no idea how to han-dle real trouble, real adversity.

"I, on the other hand, expect disaster from the start, know how to handle calamity from many rehearsals. Every day is a new adventure for muddlers. It is more exciting not knowing exactly what is going to happen next —surely the best training for life.

"It is always engineers who are saying something can't be done. Not knowing better, muddlers are the ones who give it a rip no matter what. Engineers may build the conveniences of our world but muddlers are always the ones who take the first risky steps. Was it an engineer who first thought he might be able to ride a horse? Was it an engineer who made the first snowshoes (after see-ing a ptarmigan's feet)? Or, saw a canoe in a birch tree? No, it was a muddler in every instance."

Chapter 5

OPENING AND CLOSING THE CABIN

There is something that should be said right away about cabin work. It knows no season. It never stops. At the opening and closing of the cabin it intensifies and diversifies, but there is no work-free season. I think most cabin owners are putterers and they look forward to all the little tasks that need doing. Locks to fix, new steps for the tool shed, rollers straightened on the boat ramp, shelves for the bedroom closet, the list is endless and all the projects never get done.

But, no matter, opening up the cabin in spring is like another New Year's, an exciting time of renewal. In spite of the chores to be done, it means another season of loafing, fishing, reading, puttering and all that good summer stuff is about to begin. Some tasks will be put off until next year and that's OK, but others can't be ignored.

Opening-up chores at the cabin in the spring are so numerous that it is best to make out a list before arrival and spend the next week or so whittling it down. With the popularity of cross country skiing, snowshoeing, dogsledding and other winter sports, many owners use their cabins more often in the winter months now, but in this part of the country the cabin season usually begins in earnest about mid-

May to coincide with the opening of the fishing season. It is often still chilly at this time of year, so one of the first chores will be to clean up all the dead branches that have fallen from the trees around the cabin during the winter and make a small fire in the wood stove to take the chill off the frosty mornings as well as to tidy up the property. People who live in town turn up the thermostat, but building a fire in a wood stove and basking in its heat ramps up the coziness factor in a way the thermostat never can. I think part of the fire's appeal is that it affects more of the senses than the thermostat. The feeling of heat is there of course, but one sees the dance of the flames, smells the aroma of burning wood and hears the crackle of dry branches burning for an immediate multi-sensory gratification. We only use the down and dead wood for these fires because we have a "no cut" rule that applies to all our living trees. When we built our carport in a fairly open spot full of blowdown stumps and branches near the driveway, Mike Lande, the builder, cleared the area and then sandwiched the carport into the cleared space that should have fit, but didn't quite. His creative carpentry resulted in notching the roof overhang to accommodate the two mature cedars rather than downsizing the carport.

While picking up those chunks and branches, I always check the game trails going through the back of the property for deer or moose antlers. They are usually cast in January near the trails as the bucks rub their sore antlers on trees or rocks and sometimes leave them in the snow at trailside, where the mice and other rodents usually chew on them for the calcium and other minerals.

Once in a while I get lucky and find an antler that is still in good shape. It doesn't take too long for deer antlers to be recycled by nature, but moose antlers are sometimes found by summer hikers because they are much larger and take longer for the mice and other little critters or natural processes to use them up completely.

On this first tour of the cabin property in the spring I also hike up onto the county road to check the mailbox. Most often it is lying in the ditch. The Post Office has regulations on how far from the edge of the road to locate the mailbox so the mail person can reach it from their vehicle with a handful of mail. The problem with that is then the snowplow can reach it too, and usually after the first good snowstorm, my mailbox gets swept into the ditch and spends the winter there under the snow. This year I have set my new mailbox post into an old milk can full of sand hoping that if the snowplow whacks it, it can just be set up again in the spring without any damage being done. Kind of like a bowling pin.

High on the list of spring chores should be the eviction of winter tenants and all the evidence of their residence. Critters always use the cabin when the owner is gone. There might be squirrels in the chimney, a bear's hibernation den under the cabin or the woodshed and often, mice in the kitchen drawers or the bedding. It may take a while to get them out, or if they are gone when you arrive, they'll still leave a mess for you to clean up.

We leave mousetraps baited and set when we leave in the fall, but that creates its own set of spring problems. Often a mouse will get caught in one of the traps in the early weeks of our absence, in which case the desiccated remains have to be disposed of months later (usually down the outdoor biffy hole). Sometimes the trap doesn't kill the mouse immediately and the mouse will crawl, dragging the trap into one of its hidey-holes before it dies. Desiccated mice have almost no odor, so finding all the traps can be a problem. What all this mouse traffic means is that everything has to be washed—ledges, cupboards, the oven, everything, but the water isn't on yet, so water will have to be bucketed up from the lake, a chore we hadn't planned on.

The next task is turning the water system on and for us that is always a time of surprises, mostly unpleasant. I don't remember exactly, but there may have been one or two springs in the last 25 years when the water system worked when it was first turned on. The most frequent malfunction is a burst pipe, which becomes apparent when the pressure gauge gives a little jump as the switch is turned on and then slowly sinks down to the very low end. It also means there is water spraying out somewhere along the system, hopefully not inside the walls. When this happens, it is usually because there was a little bit of water remaining somewhere in the pipe after the water was shut off in the fall and it froze there, expanding and splitting the pipe. Usually the pipes that burst are those unprotected ones running under the cabin, which is on footings, and open to the winter winds. When they burst, it means gathering up the soldering equipment, lying down and inching along under the cabin until the leak is found and repaired. I usually plead claustrophobia and try to get Les to do it.

Last spring we witnessed a brand new burst pipe problem that none of us had ever seen before. We had a two-inch tear in a shower pipe at about eye level in the bathroom wall but none of us could figure how water could stand in a vertical pipe without draining down. A suggestion was offered by one of my neighborhood plumbing "experts." Pipes often seem to have a lot of air in them. That's what all the clanking is about when the water is turned on. Somehow or other, he thought, an air bubble got trapped in the pipe coming down from the shower in our bathroom wall. Obeying a fundamental law of physics, the air bubble created a vacuum, held water in the pipe and when the big freeze came, blooey! went the pipe inside the wall when the water was turned on in the spring and the resulting spray inundated the bathroom. That seemed to be as good a suggestion as anyone could offer. It has gotten to the point where we speculate in the spring what the annual water disaster will be when we turn the pump on. It has always been manageable due to the good help of Les as long as the problem is in the interior system. I live in terror of the day when the 100-foot hose on the bottom of the lake springs a leak or the pump blows because it is submersed in 18 feet of water and I'll have to haul all that paraphernalia up on shore, or else locate a boat over the pump and pull it up with a grappling hook.

Since the Storm of the Century in 1999, which has created some serious wildfire hazards, we now have equipment that adds a whole new dimension to the challenges faced by the neighborhood water problem solvers. It is the wildfire sprinkler system that must be turned on in spring and turned off in fall. Before the Ham Lake Fire of 2007, there were about 250 residences and businesses along the Gunflint Trail which had these sprinkler systems. Now most cabin owners realize it is a good investment, compared to building a new cabin. This system consists of a series (depending on how big the property to be covered with water is) of large sprinklers connected by hose from a pump whose intake is anchored in the lake. When the gas or auxiliary propane engine is started, the pump begins sucking up lake water, the big arms of the sprinkler system start turning and soon the cabin, woodshed, outhouse and surrounding property are inundated with water. If a wildfire is reported nearby, we are to turn on our pumping system, which will run for several hours using both motors while we evacuate. Often at the springtime turn-on, the hose connections leak, the engine won't start, a fitting or valve has frozen and split, the lake level has altered the intake, or any of a dozen other catastrophes will occur which add to the problems of opening the cabin for the summer.

The sure sign the season has begun is when the dock is put in. The dock is the fourth requisite part of the cabin cluster construct—the cabin, the woodshed, the outhouse and the dock. The dock is important for a variety of reasons. It is the lake access. It is for swimming and fishing and tying the boat to. But, perhaps most important it is the "spare room." This is where sunbathing, partying and picnicking happen and where the kids play. It is literally the activity center of the cabin complex. Our dock is the place we watch the spectacular Gunflint sunsets, drink our early morning coffee while watching the pastel morning mists spiral toward the rising sun or, on inky nights, track satellites, gasp under Perseid meteor showers or stare breathlessly as curtains of multi-colored northern lights waver and vibrate across the black dome of sky.

Our dock is a large, square floating dock made of unpainted wood, and built by Mike, the builder who makes them for many cabin owners in this neighborhood. Our shore is a jumble of very large boulders, which makes impractical the popular dock with large front wheels that is easily rolled in and out of the lake each year. I have tried one of those, but the wheels get stuck among the boulders and the dock is immobilized. Steel makes the strongest dock but it is heavy, hot on the feet and rusts where the paint chips off. Aluminum is a fine dock material because it is light, easy to move around and free of rust problems. It is best in a quiet bay or on a lee shore, where there is little wind or wave action. But we are on a windward shore raked by the strong prevailing westerlies that go whistling down the lake's eight-mile length and which, I'm afraid, would pretzelize an aluminum dock. The floating dock, roped to steel pins driven deep into the boulders and the ramp anchored to shore, just bobs like a cork in the high wind.

Years ago, our neighbors Katie Lush and her husband Cliff flew a floatplane out of Gunflint, and they had a cut dug into the lakeshore in which they anchored their plane. They sold their plane long ago and the cut is not used anymore so Katie kindly lets us use it to store the dock over the winter. We just unhook everything and push the dock down there with a motorboat, tie it to some trees and let it freeze in for the winter, retrieving it the same way in spring.

Getting the boat ramp or lift in shape is the next chore and it is pretty much of a no-brainer, except for the design/engineering of the boat ramp, which has become almost a folk art here. The main reason for this is that each shore is a little different, boat sizes differ and the functions of the boats and ramp differ. For example, a pontoon boat owner will usually want a much wider walkway area than a fishing boat owner because he needs to load chairs, barbecue grills, coolers and all manner of large gear onto his boat. Fishing boats now have live wells, rod holders, ice chests, depth finders and other electronics, so all the fisherman needs to bring aboard is his tackle box and lunch, so his boat ramp can be very simple. Other, fancier ramps have umbrellas and awnings, colorful wind socks, stairways and all manner of décor and devices. In the olden days, log cribs filled with rocks were built out into the lake to hold the boat and provide a walking platform. They withstood frost and the ferocity of storms. Also, some cabin owners cut slots a little larger than their boat into the shore and lined them with logs. They had a neat little slip or "bay" which contained the boat and they could just step into it and push off from the ground. As the DNR is now very fussy about altering shorelines, these types of boat ramps, docks and cuts are illegal, but several old-timers' cabins still have them as they are grandfathered in. We have the simple plank and roller, fisherman's-type boat ramp which just sits there year-round, so doesn't require any special springtime or fall effort.

Cabin owners who have the insulated metal stove pipes with the little conical cap on them just clean out the stove for the winter, but those with masonry chimneys usually put a piece of tin with a heavy rock over the chimney opening to prevent critters (squirrels, martens, fishers, etc.) from coming down the flue and wreaking havoc in the cabin, which happens often when they discover they have no way out.

The water system also needs some autumn care. Shutting it down is simply a matter of turning switches and breaking unions, but the piping system must receive special attention for winter to avoid those pesky burst pipes. Probably the best way to be sure there are no little pockets of water anywhere in the system is to thoroughly dry it out by blowing air through the system with an air compressor. It is best to insert the compressor hose into the pipes at several locations and let it run for at least a half hour in each entry point. I always pour a cup of anti-freeze into the drains and the toilet. Some fill their entire system with anti-freeze and flush it completely in the spring. This will guarantee the system will stay frost free, but I am very skitzy about anti-freeze in drinking water, so I just use it for the toilet and drains. There is a product on the market that many use now. It is a newly formulated solution of anti-freeze that is used in RVs and mobile homes and is claimed to be much safer. The sprinkler system also requires a necessary fall chore. It must be drained, of course, the anchored intake taken up from the lake and the many connections broken, drained and rejoined. Most of those connections sit on the ground and if they are not re-joined carefully, mice, chipmunks and other little critters will run in and make cozy winter homes in the hoses. After draining water from the hoses and the fuel from the engine in the fall, the system is ready for winter. Shutting up the old cabin for the winter is kind of a sad time, but not nearly so sad as heading back to town.

Mostly, the closing-up-the-cabin-in-fall list is just a matter of reversing the spring chore list, but there are a few items which should be attended to such as a benediction memorializing another season at the cabin. An appropriate one was provided by Marilyn Heltzer writing in the Opinion Pages of the *Minneapolis Tribune*:

"There should be a ceremony for this. There should

be a much worn leather bound book with readings, scripture and songs to celebrate and mourn this day. Closing down the cabin each year marks off my life as surely as Christmas and Easter, or even baptisms and funerals, Yes, I need a ceremony here, a prayer of thanks for my dead saints. A psalm of praise for the red pines and the sturdy old cabin. A song about the voices of children jumping off the dock in the hot sunshine, with a second verse about Kool Aid and cookies and a third about a mess of perch brought in from a twilight fishing trip . . . this beach is deserted, all the other boats and docks up and down the shore have been pulled in. I'll just stand here for a few moments . . ."

Cabin Journal Note:—
Down at the east end of the lake, the two-mile-long Gunflint River connects the big lake with Little Gunflint Lake, North Lake and on down the Boundary Waters to Lake Superior. Over the years this little river has been a favorite dam site for beavers. The Minnesota DNR tries to keep the channel clear by blowing the dams up with dynamite when needed. This is effective, but it sometimes doesn't last too long. The busy beavers are often right back at it as soon as the crew leaves. A couple years ago this got to be a real competition. The beavers would build a dam; the conservation officers would blow it sky high; the beavers would build another dam and again the officers would bring in more dynamite. After a few weeks of this one of my neighbors painted a neat sign and stuck it in the brush dam. It read:

BEAVERS–3
DNR–0

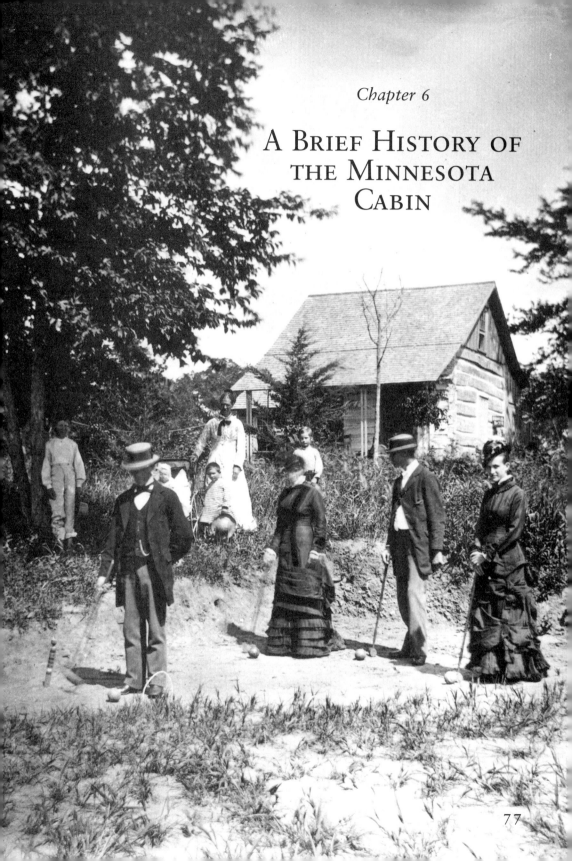

Chapter 6

A Brief History of the Minnesota Cabin

Before the Civil War, Southern plantation owners sent their families upriver to escape the extreme heat of southern summers. Their cabins were built in the Hiawatha Valley on both sides of the Mississippi River between the Twin Cities and Winona. These were largely wealthy people and the summer social season was a busy one. Frontenac, Minnesota, was known as the Newport of the North in those days. Their cabins were called "dogtrots," which are described by Mulfinger and Davis in The Cabin: "Traditionally, the dogtrot is two buildings, or two halves of a building, that are separated by an open breezeway covered by an extended gable roof. The breezeway, or open center hall, allows air circulation, a place for the dogs and provides an outdoor area that is protected from the weather—and, most important, the broiling southern sun." None of the cabins, or photos of them, are left, but this watercolor painting by artist Edwin Whitefield shows one of the dogtrot cabins near Bay City, Wis. from the 1840s.
(Minnesota Historical Society)

On the previous page: Fun and Games at the Cabin—1880
(Minnesota Historical Society)

To understand a statewide social phenomenon as big as Minnesota's century long love affair with their cabins, it will be helpful to have the perspective of history to understand how this experience got started and how it has grown.

One of the first anomalies encountered by the researcher into the history of Minnesota cabins will be to puzzle out the difference between a cabin and a cottage. The question seems to be purely academic because the words are synonymous and used interchangeably, but *Webster's Third International Dictionary* makes a rather questionable stab at differentiating:

Cottage—The dwelling of a rural laborer; A small structure built as a temporary shelter typically for shepherds or hunters; a detached, no more than two-story, frame house designed typically for summer use.

Cabin—A small, low roofed, one-story dwelling built as a home by early settlers of the North American western frontier, or by mountain folk, or suitable for overnight lodging by tourists.

There is a glimmer of distinction in that dictionary reading. The cabin seems to be a dwelling of "mountain folk" or "settlers of the North American western frontier," hence an American phenomenon, as opposed to the European cottage. Not contradictory, but a little different point of view is this note from Shirley Peruniak of the Ontario Parks Department and author of *An Illustrated History of Quetico Provincial Park.* She says, "In southeastern Ontario, people refer to 'cottages' and one seldom ever hears the word 'cabin'."

Another definition comes from Minneapolis architect Chilson D. Aldrich, who had the reputation of being the only major architect in the country who specialized in the construction of log buildings. He wrote a book, *The Real Log Cabin*, in 1928, which was updated and expanded by Harry Drabik, of Hovland, in 1994. In the book Aldrich takes the position that a cottage is a frame building covered with board siding and that a cabin is built of logs.

From Mulfinger and Davis's *The Cabin*, comes this introduction to cabin history.

"European settlers were the first to build cabins in North America—simple cubes or rectangles constructed much as their ancestors had built them. The size of available trees and the length and weight of a log two people could carry determined the modest size of the earliest cabins, usually one room wide and two rooms deep. Gently pitched roofs were easy to build, shed rain and snow and provided enough room upstairs for a loft where children slept or where the family's few possessions were stored."

These first homes were of logs from the nearby forest. The evolution of those first log houses to the recreational log cabin to the present elegant log homes is an interesting one. In Minnesota that growth was undoubtedly inspired by the art of Finnish log work and the adaptation of traditional Finnish building design forms which featured such innovations as large log buttresses, chinkless walls, double notched corners and under-the-roof firewood storage areas. In *Testaments in Wood* author Eric Paddock says:

"The log walled houses, barns and saunas reflect the adaptation of traditional Finnish forms dating from the

This 1863 homesteader's cabin exhibits some of the design and construction features of the family recreational cabin which was to follow for over 100 years—logs from the nearby forest, a tarpaper underlayment for the cedar shake roof, a clothesline strung between trees, probably a loft upstairs for the kids' beds, and most interesting, the long, sloping plank gutters angled to catch rainwater in large barrels, a popular device with many modern cabin owners.

(Minnesota Historical Society)

What started the cabin movement in Minnesota was probably the "trapper's shack," a small, hastily built shelter in which to keep supplies and serve as a temporary shelter for the trapper while on his winter rounds clerking his traps. They were usually constructed about a day's snowshoe journey apart. It was always small, built to serve fundamental needs and made of logs one man could cut and drag from the nearby forest. This one has some luxury touches like windows and mud chinking so it must have been used more often than many of the traditional trapper's cabins.

(Cook County Historical Society)

Middle Ages to the climate, materials and agriculture of northern Minnesota."

By the turn of the twentieth century, framed cabins sided with milled lumber had replaced the log cabin, but tradition, adaptability, beauty and insulating quality still make logs a popular cabin building material.

For a close look at the very beginnings of Minnesota cabins we have to go back to pre-Civil War days. In *A Place at the Lake*, by Paul Larson, it says: "Epidemics of malaria and cholera were already (1840s and '50s) driving those who could afford it to more northerly climes for the summer time." Prior to the Civil War many wealthy southern families came up the Mississippi River by steamboat to the cooler regions of Minnesota to escape the miasmal heat of their native states.

Cities on the Mississippi River (St. Anthony, Hastings, Red Wing and Frontenac, which became known as the " Newport of the Northwest") were really the first to become tourist towns in Minnesota, as wealthy southern families built cabins on the river in those areas. Many of these were the traditional Southern dog-trot cabins which looked like two cabins in tandem connected by a breezeway, where the dogs lived. Cooking was done in the smaller cabin and the larger cabin was divided into sleeping and living quarters.

In *The Fashionable Tour*, by Theodore Blegen in the fall 1939 issue of *Minnesota History* quarterly magazine, he quotes James Goodhue, the early and legendary editor of *The Minnesota Pioneer*, whom he says "often became

Finnish designed and built cabins always feature little touches that identify the signature "Finnish built." This neat little one person cabin is configured to provide "under the roof" storage for fire wood, eliminating the need for a trip to the woodshed in cold weather. The logs of Finnish farmhouses and cabins fit together so snugly, no chinking was required.
(John Henricksson)

intoxicated with his own superlatives." Goodhue pictured "the miserable life of a southern planter and his debilitated wife and pale children, almost gasping for breath."

Goodhue went on to say in the July 22, 1852 issue of *The Pioneer*, that "A month in Minnesota in dog days is worth a whole year anyplace else and we confidently see the time when all families of leisure down South from the Gulf of Mexico on up will make their regular summer hegira to our territory and when hundreds of the most opulent from these regions will build delightful cottages on the borders of our ten thousand lakes and ornament their grounds with all that is tasteful in shrubbery and horticulture for a summer retreat."

Because of the myriad lakes in what is now the Twin Cities area of Minneapolis and St. Paul and their burgeoning population, the lakes of the metropolitan region became cabinized next.

The first recorded sighting of Lake Minnetonka, near Minneapolis, which was to become the greatest tourist draw in the state, was in 1822 when Josiah Snelling's son Joseph and a friend followed Minnehaha Creek from the falls to its source. Thirty years later in the mid-1850s, Simon Stevens and Calvin Tuttle walked the lake in the wintertime and "The *St. Anthony Express* trumpeted their discoveries in a pair of stories," according to Larson. By 1870 there were many cottages and grand hotels on the lake.

White Bear Lake, ten miles north of St. Paul, was the next cabin neighborhood to develop in Minnesota. In 1890 the *St. Paul Pioneer Press*, in a rhapsodic seizure, noted:

"White Bear Lake sits like a sapphire set about with emeralds, a dazzling brooch which rises and falls upon

Many cabin builders, especially those who utilize logs from trees grown on the property, often balsam-fir, which are smaller and have more taper than spruce or pine, place the logs alternating vertically when the cabin is framed. The logs are then cut into 8 foot lengths, lapped on  *the bottom and cut flat on top for quick and effective siding. One old time cabin builder said they called them "peg cabins" and that they used "anything that looked like a stick."* (Cook County Historical Society)

Abandonment is the fate of many cabins, CCC camps, farms, logging and mining camps throughout the north. Sometimes whole communities disappear. For whatever reasons, the owner(s) just walk away and leave the buildings to the elements and decay. At 50 years the cabin is disintegrating. The yard and the road are overgrown with a new forest. At 100 years all wood has rotted and crumbled. There is perhaps an outline of base timbers left and only a low spot in the tree line horizon to hint at the cabin location. (John Henricksson)

This Kentucky-style cabin built in 1936 of still solid white spruce logs features some renovations by the current owner, but the twin gable signature still identifies the mark of its designer and builder, Walt Yocum, who came to the northwoods from his native Kentucky. (John Henricksson)

sweet nature's bosom, overlooked by her blue eyes, brightened by her sunny smiles and swept by her fragrant sighs." That was enough to draw hundreds of new residents to its banked and wooded shores, which were "graced throughout with imposing and picturesque cottages, where dwell, during the summer months, many of St. Paul's estimable and wealthy people."

All of this was before the invention of the automobile and the construction of highways, so cabin owners and vacationers had to rely on the horse and wagon and later, the railroad, or perhaps both to get "up to the lake."

Minnesota's lakes and rivers provided the first means of transportation for settlers and trade goods. In the middle of the eighteenth century, Dakota Indians brought the first horses to the upper plains for use as beasts of burden and transportation. In the early 1800s the Red River Oxcart Trail ran from the settlements around Pembina to St. Paul. Perhaps the earliest road in the state was a trail used before 1816 by British soldiers between Grand Portage and Fort Charlotte on the Pigeon River.

In May of 1849 stagecoach service started between Stillwater and St. Paul. The steamboat "Alhambra" brought the first steam locomotive, the "William Crooks," to Minnesota in 1861. Five years later the state was linked to Chicago by rail. By 1929 the number of miles of track in Minnesota peaked at 5,410 miles. It went down from there due to the Depression, competition from motor carriers, depletion of the forests and the bankruptcy of railroad companies. But for years, the railroads brought the tourists to Minnesota.

In Susan Hawkinson's *Timber Connections*, she tells how the vacation trip was made to the Itasca County area on the western edge of the Arrowhead in the early twentieth century: ". . . Irv Martin established a modest beachfront log cabin at the north end of Trout Lake . . . Two or three years later McAlpine's (lumber) camp closed, leaving Martin ideally positioned as the industry in the area turned from logging to tourism."

Louis Ireton, a Cincinnati lawyer, heard about the great fishing in the Grand Rapids area. Ireton posted a letter to Martin reserving two cabins for his family for the next summer. After a fatiguing train trip from Cincinnati to Grand Rapids that following year, the Ireton family was met by Ernie Poland at the train station. His livery service extended as far as Taylor's Landing at the south end of Wabana Lake, where Irv Martin waited on shore with his motor launch to ferry the family through the lake chain to Trout Lake. An hour later Martin cut the motor and coasted to a stop alongside his dock. Out stepped the Iretons with their carpetbag trunk to begin a leisurely month casting for fish. The family most often chose Spider Lake for outings, landing bass for their noon picnics. The Iretons returned to Trout Lake the next two summers, and purchased property on the hillside above Martins."

In Larson's history, *A Place at the Lake*, we learn that what was then called "The Western Crescent, a route of three railroads, running west from the Twin Cities through Kandiyohi County then turning north curving through Glenwood, Alexandria and Detroit Lakes before hooking northeast to Bemidji" along the route of the Northern Pacific, the Manitoba Road and eventually the Soo Line, was the next popular summer cabin area to develop in the 1870s and '80s. "Trainloads of tourists camped, cottaged and stayed at resorts on lakes in this grand wild parkland for a full generation before the invention of the automobile." Detroit Lakes was the first town in northern Minnesota to develop a summer community.

Boys' and Girls' camps were also an important element in the family decision to build their cabin in northern Minnesota. In an article on Minnesota Boys' and Girls' camps in the summer of 2002 issue of *Minnesota History*, Abigail A. Van Slyck writes:

"Summer camps began as one component of a back to nature trend that developed in Anglo-American culture in the last quarter of the nineteenth century. Summer camps offered urban dwellers contact with nature, which

The cabin above, a new 25' by 35' rectangular "box" with a sloping roof and horizontal log siding, is the prototype Minnesota family cabin. There are thousands of them, of various ages, all over the state. The features of the newer ones are all utilities, indoor plumbing, insulation, septic systems, metal roofs and sun decks, but the basic design has remained much the same . . . (John Henricksson) *Below is the same style cabin a century earlier, very much alike in shape and size, built by Norwegian immigrant Emil Edison, at Castle Danger on the North Shore of Lake Superior in 1910. Originally it was a bark-on log cabin, but at some point it was covered with traditional lap siding and utilities installed for Star Harbor Resort at Castle Danger, Minnesota, the first "cabin type" resort in the state. It was given to the Minnesota Historical Society by the owners, the Byrnes family, and is presently undergoing renovation for display.* (Minnesota Historical Society)

Here's an example of creative problem solving you probably couldn't get away with in town . . . the cabin owner's answer to inadequate interior space for all the large items he wanted to keep around. He has created a decorative/utilitarian exterior storage space . . . or is it a museum display?
(John Henricksson)

was believed to be an important antidote to the evils of the industrialized city. For children such contact was considered especially important.

"Indeed Victorian ideology held that the city threatened the very physical health of children and their mothers. The conditions that attracted so many Victorian families to Minnesota's grand summer resorts and children's camps in the last quarter of the nineteenth century made the state ideal for this new kind of experience."

Among the early camps for youngsters were Camp Icaghowan, on Green Lake near Chicago City, a YMCA camp founded in 1908; Camp Lincoln on Lake Hubert, near Brainerd in 1909; Camp Mishiwaka on Lake

Pokegama near Grand Rapids, founded in 1910; Camp Ojakita, a Campfire Girls camp founded in 1926 on Green Lake near Spicer; Camp Lakamaga, founded in 1927 on Big Marine Lake near Marine on St. Croix; and Camp Warren, a YMCA camp on Half Moon Lake in St. Louis County in 1928.

Van Slyck speculates that the conditions that attracted so many families to Minnesota made the state an ideal setting for this new kind of experience for the children. The family liked the area and the camp so well they decided to build their vacation cabin nearby.

The invention of the automobile and the construction of the highway system started the century-long migration of Minnesota families from their house in town "up to the lake" and the summer cabin. In 1896 the first gas-powered automobiles were manufactured. The Duryea was seen on Minnesota roads early in the century. Those first cars had a joystick for steering until Packard introduced the steering wheel in 1900. The Ford Motor Company was formed in 1903 and introduced the Model T that same year. A touring car of that popular model was introduced in 1908. These were quickly followed by Buick and Chevrolet. Ford opened its Minneapolis plant in 1912 and made 12 cars a day.

The state only had 75 miles of paved roads then. The horse remained the people's engine. There were 17 million of them in America in 1903, and about 23,000 cars. But in 1921, the Minnesota Department of Highways began building the trunk highway system and by 1925 more than 500,000 vehicles were registered in Minnesota and in that year 15 million passengers traveled its roads. In 1926 a system of numbered highways was established, and the first state highway maps were published in 1919.

By 1910 cars were responsible for the opening of family cabins, summer camps, and resorts in Minnesota's north country and by 1920 when the North Shore Drive along Lake Superior was straightened, surfaced and opened to tourist travel, the Arrowhead region became a popular tourist destination.

In a large bay of the 1500 Mississippi Building, the Minnesota Historical Society's storage facility, a forlorn old cabin sits up on blocks patiently waiting to be rehabilitated. It has been sitting there for quite a while because the Society, which is always woefully short of budget and staff, hasn't yet prioritized the task of returning it to its 1910 glory.

The cabin is the traditional 16 by 35-foot one-room rectangle, its blue-painted pine siding boards covering the original unpeeled logs. It was built by Norwegian immigrant Emil Edison in 1910 for its original occupants, railroad executives who came to monitor the building of the railroad at Two Harbors and who needed a place to stay other than a tent. Edison also built the Rustic Inn Restaurant across Highway 61, which is still in business today. According to a Lake County Historical Society file, "The executives soon began bringing their families and other families began building cabins nearby." This is typical of the way cabin neighborhoods grew. Pals' Cove, up the North Shore near Hovland, and the Encampment Forest cabin settlement, down the Shore, are good examples of this trend from the early part of the twentieth century.

*This cabin epitomizes architect-author Dale Mulfinger's philosophy that a
cabin should not challenge the landscape in which it is located. He said:
"Respecting the environment is only part of the unspoken code of cabin
building. Another part is that no matter where it is built and whatever it
is built of, a cabin should enhance the landscape, not overpower it. The
best cabins don't overwhelm the land, they blend into it. Cabins should
look as though they grew out of the site."* (William O. Lyders)

This collection of cabins at Castle Danger became
Star Harbor, the first cabin resort on the North Shore
(Lutsen, established earlier, was a resort hotel) and is now
the site of the elegant Grand Superior Lodge. Travelers
who have been going up and down the North Shore drive
for years will remember the Edison-carved statue of Jiggs
at the gate, who tipped his top hat to passersby for many
years at the Star Harbor entrance.

Some cabin owners have heeded the instructions from FIREWISE, a national program sponsored by the U.S. Forest Service and operated locally by DNR by volunteers from the community and the fire department. The goal is to educate cabin owners on how to protect their property from wildfires. This cabin, which suffered only some broken window damage from the extreme heat, was surrounded by the Ham Lake Fire but escaped serious damage because the owner had paid close attention to the FIREWISE cautions—he cleared a forty foot area of brush around the cabin, installed a metal roof and skirted the cabin which is on footings so no burning firebrands could be blown underneaeth and start a fire there. (John Henricksson)

The interior of the cabin has always been its richest treasure and most informative artifact. It has always been the repository of all the things nobody really wanted around the house. Whenever a questionable gift was unwrapped at Christmastime, someone was bound to say, "Well, we can always use it up at the cabin." And so, over the years, most cabins have become the final resting place of many items of questionable taste. Again, from *The Cabin*:

"Because they are often passed down through families, cabins tend to collect bits and pieces from everybody who came before. Wooden floors record the scuffs and scratches of generations . . . little caches of stuff collected over generations by cabin children show up now and then. Grownups leave their marks too. A hand-pieced quilt, old fishing rods, furniture that reached its prime back when only women wore earrings . . . The bare lightbulb fits just fine with the secondhand refrigerator. The coffeepot and iron skillet are preferred kitchen utensils."

When the Minnesota Historical Society took possession of the cabin, they made a thorough inventory of its contents and found some of these items which fit the family castoff pattern. Here are a few of them:

"Three rectangular curtain panels of white cotton cretonne each with a florid floral print with very large faded pink flower (possibly rhododendron), encircled by yellow and mauve daisies, and tropical foliage."

"Rectangular bath mat of light aqua chenille with swimming swans appliqué at either end."

"Oval porcelain platter, cream-colored glaze, with multi-colored underglaze with floral print at center."

"Overstuffed sofa covered with medium blue, white, green and tan upholstery in variegated weave with three button tufts."

"Electric toaster with elongated octagonal base, vented chrome sides with black Bakelite knobs open to accommodate one slice next to heating element. Black and white striped electric cord."

"Rectangular valance of white cotton cretonne with basket of pink flowers and scissors on fringed rug alternating with white-petaled flower in watering can."

Some of these items would be bizarre in the New Suburbia of the present North Shore, but somehow in the less upscale areas of northern Minnesota where there are still old family cabins, they are considered heritage items.

Chief Curator and Head of Museum Collections for the Minnesota Historical Society, Marcia Anderson, said recently:

"The Edison cabin, its contents and its associated activities have been an important part of Minnesota's social history for nearly a century and a half. Whether it belonged to a friend, to a resort or the family, time at the cabin has always been the quality time of family life here. We are grateful to the Byrnes family of Castle Danger for making this cabin available and we hope its display will renew warm memories for all Minnesotans."

Cabin Journal Note:—
The Gunflint Trail, which pre-dated the North Shore Drive, was originally built because extensive mining was anticipated near the Canadian border. It has been the Gunflint Trail almost as far back as living memory goes but was

first known as the Gunflint Wagon Road. Then in the early 1920s it was known as the "Jake Preus Highway," and went from Grand Marais to Poplar Lake, or Milepost 34. J.A.O. Preus was the governor of Minnesota from 1921 to 1925, and built his summer headquarters on the Ontario side of Gunflint Lake, a cabin complex his descendants maintained for many years. The entire nine-cabin enclave was completely destroyed in the Ham Lake Fire of 2007, but is now being rebuilt. No one knows who named it the Gunflint Trail, or when the name was adopted. Gunflint Trail historian Sue Kerfoot noted that it began to appear in the Cook County *News- Herald* by that name sometime in the mid-twenties.

Chapter 7

Mice—Our Constant Companions

Mice have created the ultimate cabin democracy. Every cabin owner has them. Like moss on the roof or mosquitoes, they go with the territory.

We have a veritable mouse menagerie here: the deer mouse and red-backed vole are most common, but we also see substantial populations of meadow voles, white-footed mice, woodland jumping mice and the most widely distributed of all, the house mouse, even though that particular specie is only supposed to be a problem in areas of human habitation and not in forested land. Perhaps because we are a human habitation in the forest, the house mouse has decided that we qualify. This European immigrant is grayish-brown and is about 5 inches long, including the tail. They have many litters during the year and each litter has from 3 to 16 mouselings. We have both the tiny masked and short-tailed shrews in the woods around the cabin, but they are carnivores and there is little in the cabin to interest them, so they don't bother us.

Most often in residence at the cabin is the deer mouse. Even though I wouldn't have a trapped specimen to identify by their bi-colored tail, I could tell what it was scrabbling around up in the bedroom ceiling because deer mice are arboreal and are the only mice who can climb trees and walls quite easily with the aid of their long stiff tails, so I have to set the traps in high places. I have gotten dozens of deer mice in specially-built little trap holders set from a ladder where the ceiling joins the walls. When I do sometimes get one behind the stove or on the bottom shelf of the cupboard, it will most often be a house mouse.

The woodland deer mouse is found most often in coniferous or mixed woodlands, has round ears and a white belly (Tom and Jerry are deer mice), is strictly nocturnal and lives only about a year in the wild (eight years in captivity). We hear them because they squeak and scramble. Deer mice do not gnaw wood noisily like most other mice. For nest material they prefer afghan fringes, wool sweaters and insulation bats. The toilet paper in the outhouse often hangs in long shreds, so I suspect there are house mice living out there.

We have waves of mouse invasions. We will be mouse free for a month or more; no droppings, no night noises, no mice in the traps. Then suddenly, there is a mouse population explosion. A paper-lined dresser drawer in the small bedroom or the top of the stove seems to serve as the community latrine. Scurrying noises trace their wall and ceiling trails and the traps fill regularly with an almost nightly precision. Julie found one snoozing in a frying pan in the stove drawer one day and it was so groggy from the oven heat it hardly wiggled as she hurried outside to dump the pan.

The snap of a trap going off calls for a trip to the mouse re-cycling table out in back where the owls and the pine martens always seem to be waiting. Regardless of how many mice I dump out there at night, the table is always clear in the morning. I did see a raven swoop in one day, pick up the mouse in its beak and fly off, but most of them disappear at night, so I suspect the nocturnal predators.

Then suddenly there are no mice in the cabin for several weeks. But we know it will start again. It isn't weather changes or birth cycles or an increase in predator populations. There seems to be no reason for these periodic invasions. But they happen with great regularity and have for over twenty five years. Plugging all holes and cracks to keep the cabin mouse-free is, of course, the obvious but frustrating solution.

"Build them out," the building contractors say. That sounds simple enough, but it assumes that you can find or eliminate all the possible one-quarter-inch places a mouse can get in. That can be a knothole, a crack, the little space behind a shingle, or under roofing. It can be under a door that doesn't fit perfectly or a frayed spot in a screen. One of the first and worst mouse entrances to a cabin is the holes drilled into the floor for water pipes to enter: sinks, showers, toilets, etc. The pipe must fit very tightly or Mr. Mouse will lead his extended family up and into the cabin when you aren't looking.

There are three very effective mouse hole stuffer-uppers: steel wool, aluminum foil and a fast hardening foam spray available at any hardware store. Mice hate steel wool and aluminum foil and will make no attempt to pull it out or sneak in next to it. The foam is "an expanding sealant under pressure which insulates, seals, fills, stops drafts and pests." It works great for barricading the cabin from mouse invasions. The only problem is finding all the holes. Our cabin juts out from sloping rock and the mice have been smart enough to locate their entry holes almost at the point where the cabin joins the rock. There is no way I can get at that spot with the foam can, or even see the entry to the mouse highways that apparently criss-cross the interior cabin walls. It goes without saying that doors and windows must fit tightly, and remember. Don't ever leave any doors open. Not just for a minute. Ever!

Once they are in, some form of trapping is called for and there is a broad gamut of technology open to the cabin owner, from the primitive but effective FrankPlank to an electronic device ($32.50) that sprays the area with ultrasonic sounds, well above the range of human hearing, and drives the mice wacko. There is a problem here. These waves are directional and do not sneak around behind furniture and into mouse holes. As a result they work for only a couple days. The mice wise up to them fast and soon are going about their mousey business ducking into places unreachable by the ultrasonic waves. For the heavy infestation, there is a device called a "windup trap" that has a mechanism which kicks up to 15 mice into the trap. Over the years literally hundreds of mouse-traps have been invented, among them The Mousemobile live trap, the Kitty Gotcha and my favorite antique, the Hotchkiss Five-Hole Choker. There is a Trap Collectors Society whose members pay big prices for just the right antique mousetrap.

While considering the many types of mouse traps available, that phrase about the good fortune that awaited the person "who built a better mouse trap" kept running through my head and drove me to searching for its provenance. I finally found it. It is by the transcendentalist poet Ralph Waldo Emerson:

"If a man can write a better book, preach a better sermon, or make a better mousetrap than his neighbor, though he builds his house in the woods, the world will make a beaten path to his door."

An early patent, the old-fashioned Victor Easy Set, is still probably the most effective mouse trap ever invented, even though it is so old no one can remember when Grandpa first began using it. A few years ago a slight change was made. It was probably the marketing department, under pressure to come up with something new, who suggested painting the bait pedal yellow to resemble a piece of cheese, which is ridiculous. A mouse is far too smart to mistake a piece of painted plastic for tasty Swiss cheese.

The FrankPlank is an interesting device invented by my neighbor/friend who has built many of the cabins in this area. When building our cabin, Frank had the floor and studdings in and was framing in windows when he noticed mice were running all over the floor and lumber piles. The cabin is on a slope and from the floor with the bedrooms, bathroom and closets it is two steps down into the living area. On this higher floor Frank balanced a long 1 x 2 inch board with the fulcrum, or tipping point, at the stair edge. He sprinkled shelled corn along the board and placed a high-sided cardboard carton beneath it on the living room floor. The mice would scoot along the board gleefully picking up kernels of corn until they got to the fulcrum. With the mouse's weight ahead of the fulcrum, the stick would tip foward sharply and the mouse would slide uncontrollably down the board into the box. When the box had several scrambling mice in it, Frank would take the whole thing down to the lake and empty it, set it back under the board and begin the whole process all over. We never kept track of how many mice Frank caught with this device but it must have been hundreds over the period of cabin building. There are many other devices for catching mice, but none as simple or effective as the FrankPlank.

Having lived in a cabin on the Saganaga channel for many years, Frank has had a lot of time to consider the mouse/cabin problem and has come up with several ingenious solutions. One I like involves locating one or more of the old-fashioned kapok stuffed life preservers. I expect they aren't even made any more but were very popular a few decades ago. Maybe an old boathouse or antique store might be a good place to start looking. Frank cuts a couple long slits in the canvas covering of the life preserver and places it under the cabin. He claims the mice love the coziness of the kapok and will gladly make their home there instead of breaking into the cabin.

Scattering a few hedge balls around the house is supposed to be an excellent mouse repellant, according to our friend Vicki Biggs-Anderson who swears by their effectiveness, even though I have never had her luck with them. They are a sort of fluorescent green, warty fruit available in the produce department of grocery stores and supermarkets from late August until December. Vicki thinks the odor must drive mice bonkers because when she retrieves them from under the bed and other places where she has scattered them, there are never any toothmarks on the fruit, but all the mice have vanished. Writing in the *St. Paul Pioneer Press*, Ellen Tomson enlightens us about hedge balls:

"What is this lumpy thing? A hedge ball, an inedible fruit that, when placed in the basement or kitchen, repels insects, spiders, roaches, waterbugs and rodents. At least, that's what the information sheet near the hedge ball display at the Highland Park (St. Paul) Lunds says.

"Also known as hedge apples, monkey balls, mock oranges and horse apples, hedge balls are the fruit of Osage orange trees, which were planted by farmer settlers to delineate fields.

"Evidence about the hedge ball's effectiveness as a pest deterrent is inconclusive. But generations of households have placed the fruit in their homes . . . eventually the hedge balls turn brown and shrink to the size of a walnut, but devotees says they continue to work even then."

Across the broad field of mouse trapping, I detect a sea change from cheese to peanut butter as the bait of choice. Old peanut butter is perhaps not as pungent as old cheese, but it has some distinct advantages. For one thing it is moldable like clay, and can be formed around the bait pedal making it harder for the mouse to get it all without pulling the trigger and getting whacked by that deadly metal bar. It seems to have a universal appeal to all mouse species . . . and it is much cheaper.

A three-dollar jar of peanut butter will last the trapper all season. A half-gallon jar of grape jelly left open on the cabin counter overnight will also usually produce good results. It accounted for eighteen purple, fuzzy blobs in one night for Carol, the Berry Lady.

There are glue board traps, but I see this as the penultimate cruelty to animals. Hoping for a tasty reward, the mouse steps onto the glue coated board, and unable to escape, there it starves to death or until someone comes along to put it out of its misery.

The cruelest by far is poison because, when the mouse dies from ingesting it, the corpse will likely be eaten by some predator and so the poison gets into the food chain and the mouse's death is only the beginning.

Fumigation shouldn't even be considered unless the mice are clearly winning the battle for the cabin and are about to drive the owner bonkers. It involves professional taping and sealing the building, filling it with a poison gas and leaving it alone for several days. The mice (and everything else) will all be dead and after airing it out well, you can move back in and start over. But understand, this is the final, desparate action of a distraught cabin owner whose last option is to surrender to the mice. We aren't there yet, but like most cabin owners, we do have a problem.

The thought occurs to me that maybe I have approached this whole problem wrong and haven't done enough to establish a closer détente with the mice. Mice aren't noisy or destructive like teenagers, they're cute little critters and are always cleaning themselves, licking off their whiskers and face and combing their fur with their paws. The author Helen Hoover, who lived in the cabin next door, seemed to have a great relationship with the mice. She named them all and considered them her friends.

At night she would leave hazelnut shells filled with bits of cookie, chocolate and a walnut kernel on the dining room table. Little Brownie, her favorite, would always appear for his treat at exactly the same time every night.

Old timers up here who used to get wintered in occasionally, and were starved for companionship, staved off cabin fever by welcoming the mice; feeding them, making friends and carrying on long discussions of political and philosophical matters with them. Maybe I should try their method.

Cabin Journal Note:—
This hastily scribbled note was found folded and tucked into a crack in a stump on the Alpine Lake portage. I never found out who wrote it or how the adventure ended.

I killed myself because of: (check one)

__Bit by a deer tick

__Digging a latrine in the BWCA

__Living with Doug

__All of the above

Chapter 8

BERRIES, BERRIES, BERRIES

THIS IS WILD BERRY COUNTRY. The habitat and climate seem to be just right for an annual summer crop of blueberries, raspberries, strawberries and thimbleberries. High bush cranberries and rosehips are both picked for best taste after the first touch of frost in the fall. The products are featured year-round in our pies, breads, coffee cakes, pancakes, rolls, muffins, jams, jellies, juices and on cereals and ice cream toppings. Although they are used primarily to make jelly, rose hips are also used to make a delicious tea, one of the highest sources of natural vitamin C. During World War II, there were no oranges available in England, so many mothers gathered rose hips and made a drink for their children that was rich in the important vitamin C. This, and most other information I pick up about wild berries, comes from neighbor Carol, the Gunflint Berry Lady, who spends many hours in the woods each year picking wild berries and even more in her kitchen preparing tasty berry products which we often sample.

She has also taught me about fruit leather, a pemmican-like trail food, or chewable confection, which is another gift from the Indians. Carol has a nifty juice pot which is a Finnish-made, expensive, hard-to-find device something like a large double boiler with a hose and faucet near the bottom of the colander-like inside pot. An ordinary double boiler is an alternative but it's not as good and the boiling time will be longer. To make the fruit leather Carol dumps in all the skins, seeds and pulp and lets it boil for an hour or until it turns very thick and gooey. She says you can add a little sugar or orange juice if you prefer. Pour it out in a series of long strips onto a cookie sheet and put it in a gas oven with just the pilot light on for two days, or a day on each side and dry it out until almost all the moisture is gone and it is like soft leather. Old timers who made this fruit leather as a trail food let it stay out in the sun for a couple days instead of in the oven, until it was just the right consistency. The problem with that method is rain and bugs. Stick to the stove drying and the product will be cleaner and better. The strips should be very thin, the better to be broken into whatever size pieces are needed. This is a highly nutritious trail snack and ideal for the kit bag on a canoe trip. Katie Lechter-Lyle suggests in her wonderful guide, *The Wild Berry Book*, that to store the fruit leather for a long period of time it would be a good idea to roll it up between layers of waxed paper.

Carol also saves the juice from the scarcer berries, such as ground raspberries, choke cherries or any berry or fruit she finds in small amounts, mixes them all together and makes a multi-berry, or scarce berry jam that is to die for. The Canadians make this and call it The Queen's Jam.

The blueberries and raspberries get most of the attention because they are most numerous, versatile and tasty. These berries are here in uncounted millions and depend only on the right combination of rainfall, sunlight and temperature to blossom and fruit into an unimaginable profusion. Ms. Letcher-Lyle says, "Wild berries may be the only thing on this continent found in more abundance today than when the first European settlers stepped onto our soil." She also guesses that fewer than one-tenth of one percent of wild berries are picked each year. She goes on to say that berrying is the perfect hobby. It costs nothing, it yields free food, has few perils and requires very little in the way of equipment.

Some might consider the presence of bears in the berry patch a peril, but bears are hard to avoid here because they can be anywhere. If the patch is torn up and there are piles of bear scat around, it would probably be a good idea to find another place to pick, but generally normal caution is enough. If you're alone, wear bear bells, sing loudly or talk to yourself. If there are others picking with you, carry on a lively conversation. A wilderness berry patch is the one place being loud and obstreperous is acceptable. Like most wild creatures, bears don't like to be surprised, so don't be a sneaky picker.

Perhaps one of the reasons for the abundance of raspberries now is that raspberry bushes are the first ones up and growing after timber is clearcut, burned or blown down. In the same season the trees are cleared, the bushes will be knee high, but they won't bear fruit for at least another year. Raspberries grow best in open sunlight, and the Storm of the Century in 1999 and the Ham Lake Wildfire of 2007 opened up thousands of acres to sunlight so we are now getting a superabundance of raspberries. We find a basket or tray is best for picking these berries because they are much softer than blueberries and have a tendency to moosh up if they are picked into a plastic bag. Thimbleberries, many of which are eaten by the birds, are also very soft and full of seeds, but make a good jelly and have a delicious, tart flavor.

Like gooseberries and black currants, the wild raspberries, an English import and a naturalized citizen here, are carriers of a certain stage of the blister rust in white pines. What is called locally skunk currant should be avoided. It is hairy and smells bad. The birds don't seem to care and get most of all the currants and gooseberries anyway, so not many people pick them. The red raspberries have an interesting medical history which is also reported in *The Wild Berry Book*. A substance in the leaves has been isolated by medical researchers which strengthens the uterine walls of pregnant women, and the high magnesium content is recommended to prevent miscarriage. Without previous knowledge of any of this science, an old wives' tale from colonial days advises pregnant mothers that raspberry leaf tea should be taken throughout pregnancy. Then too, the leaves are very soft so the Indians used them for toilet paper.

At first glance blueberries and huckleberries appear identical. Wrong. There is very little difference, and botanists admit you have to look very closely to see the identifiers, but they are separate species and huckleberries grow in the South and blueberries in the North.

Strawberries, which are herbs not berries, are America's favorite wild berry. They are very controversial among berry pickers. Ms. Lechter-Lyle says that "by any economic measure picking wild strawberries is a waste of time because they are so tiny, hard to pick and well hidden," although she admits "they are worth a great deal in superior flavor and pleasure." Wild strawberries are not supposed to be washed and that gives me a problem. Around here they grow primarily along roadsides because they need sandy soil and the full day's sun, but most berry books caution *not to pick* along roads because the exhaust fumes of gasoline engines and the spraying for insects by road crews spoil the berries for human consumption.

The flavor of those first wild blueberries of the summer is a pleasurable and unique taste sensation. Definitely the flavor of the season. Frozen they are still good, but those first pickings provide the sweet, but slightly acid essence of north country, totally absent in domestically raised blueberries.

Blueberrying has almost as long a history here as beaver trapping. Even though they seem to grow everywhere in good years, favorite blueberry patches are closely guarded family secrets and their locations are handed down through generations. If one of my neighbors is seen with a four-quart ice cream bucket full of big juicy blueberries, a stranger might inquire casually where he got them. I can't wait to listen in on the answer.

"Oh, these came from up around Seagull Creek near where Old Claude got lost looking for Disappointment Lake," the veteran picker may answer. Old Claude has been dead for 25 years, and no one remembers where he got lost anyway. Or, maybe, he might say, "We were picking north of the old Post Office about a mile off County 92." North of the old Post Office a mile would be right in the middle of Iron Lake.

Maybe because of the heavy forest cover, in earlier times berries weren't so plentiful because they thrive best in areas that get some sunlight. The good patches were always family secrets and the only way favorite spots were revealed was through the inheritance process. We were touched and grateful when neighbor Janna Webster moved to North Dakota to be a horse wrangler and passed her blueberry patch on to us. We have been faithful to her trust, pick all the blueberries we want every year and have never told a soul where the magic place it is. Someday we'll pass it on to a friend. That's the way it is with good blueberry patches.

The patch she directed us to is entered at the overgrown entrance to an old forest road. The power line goes through not far from the entrance and there are often good berries hidden in the long grass on the hilly spots so we stop there and pick for a few minutes. There are several places like that in the couple miles along the way to Blueberry Rock, which is the spot Janna told us about. By the time we get there our buckets are usually half full from the many stops we make along the way. It doesn't take us long to fill because this is one of those patches that are picked by stripping branches of their handsful of berries into the bucket rather than picking individual ones. Eight or ten pea-sized berries per tug is about average. Loki, the big chocolate lab, goes through the patch like a bear, head low to the ground, lower jaw open like a scoop shovel and he takes berries, leaves, twigs and all.

With this bounty it isn't an important consideration, but be prepared to have blue hands and knees because the crushed berries stain easily. Ms. Lechter-Lyle tells some wonderful berry stories, but I liked the one about the New England whaling sailors dying their clothes with blueberry juice, and hence the term Navy Blue.

Blueberry Rock itself is an unusual formation because it is the highest elevation rise in the surrounding country. Standing on top of it, I can see about a mile of clearcut scrubby beaked hazel, jack pine, young aspen and balsam fir in each direction. We could spend the entire day picking blueberries on that rock. It is completely covered with the bushes and a few stunted jack pines. It bears out what Frank the Cabin Builder told me years ago. "If you want to find blueberries up here, look for rocks and jack pines."

On the way back to the cabin, buckets filled with blueberries, we look for another hill we used to pick on this same road. It was high, surrounded by huge boulders and capped with big pines. The ground under those jack pines was covered with blueberry bushes. It has changed quite a bit since the big storm and the fire. It is practically bald now with a fringe of shattered trees on top of the boulders around the rim. It would be almost impossible to climb to the top where the bonanza bushes of big berries used to grow. But we have often stopped on our way back, looked up there and wondered if the top of that hill was still the treasure chest it used to be. Someday we're going to try it again.

When we get a bountiful harvest like we did last year, the word gets around and people flock from all over to pick berries here in the Superior National Forest. With normal berry picking techniques and the large number of pickers, that wouldn't be a problem. There are berries enough for everyone, including the bears. But there are some people who are so greedy they abuse the privilege of public land. Near the entrance to the Loon Lake Public Access on the Gunflint Trail, there is an overgrown hint of a road that I suppose someone had cut one day to a stand of trees or to a campground. Last year someone had backed a long flatbed truck trailer into that opening loaded with a dozen large, institutional coolers which a large group of pickers were filling with blueberries. They picked in that general area for several days and finally left with full coolers. I don't know whether they were picking them for a couple years' worth of their personal use or if they were selling them. In town a few days later, I was still steamed and I checked with the district ranger at the Forest Service Headquarters to see if this was legal.

"It is legal for anyone to pick berries on public land," she said. "It probably would not be legal to sell the berries, but we certainly can't stop people from picking them. They can't use mechanical pickers, but the amount they pick by hand is not restricted."

Preserving the berries is always a necessity and sometimes a problem. One never picks just enough for pancakes when they are abundant. There is something about several acres of huge blueberries bending the bushes to the ground that makes picking just a few impossible. I suppose it's greed, but I like to think I'm being provident, storing up food for the winter.

As soon as we get the berries home, we put them in a big strainer or colander and wash them well under the spray nozzle of the kitchen faucet. Then we line a cookie sheet with paper toweling and spread the berries out, picking out all the leaves, twigs and unripe berries. Then we gently pat them dry with a paper towel. When they are clean and dry, we fill small containers or bags (preferably the one-pint size) and store them in the freezer. They last well and we use them all winter in pies, coffee cakes, ice cream topping and pancakes.

Another way to preserve them is suggested by Ms. Lechter-Lyle in her book. She instructs us to boil equal parts of sugar and water together until all the sugar is dissolved into a syrup. A good storage formula is 8 parts of berries to 2 parts of syrup. Fill a plastic bag to near the top, squeeze out the remaining air and pop the berry bag into the freezer.

Bon Appetit!

Cabin Journal Note:—
There are several species of cherry trees growing wild in the woods around the neighborhood, and one of Peggy Heston's favorite times of year was when the trees were heavy with the succulent fruit. She could always be found then in the kitchen making cherry pies, cobbler and jelly. One day she was grousing to neighbor Charlie Olson, the summer home caretaker, about having to take the time to hike around in the woods, picking all the cherries and hauling the baskets back to her kitchen. Charlie, always the source of creative problem-solving ideas, grabbed his axe, went into the woods, cut down a cherry laden tree and hauled it onto Peggy's back porch.

"There you are," he said. "Now get to work on that pie you promised me."

Chapter 9

Cabin Fever?
Deal With It

IN THE "OLDEN DAYS" when autumn leaves covered the cabin roof and lacey little ice patterns could be found on the rocks along the morning shore, it was cabin closing time.

The water was shut off, a piece of tin weighted down with a rock was put over the chimney to keep the critters out, the electricity turned off, the dock and boat ramp were dragged up on shore, doors and windows securely fastened shut as another season at the cabin had come to a close and everyone headed back to town for the winter.

Today, many cabins are in use year-round. Permanent residents, cross country skiers, retirees, bird watchers, cabin/computerized business operators, fishermen, hunters, dog mushers, arts and crafts producers and others keep many cabins filled even during the harshest winter months. What with vastly improved equipment, services and communications, getting snowed in is not the threat it used to be. Old timers tell of occasionally being cabin bound for weeks before they could get out, but that doesn't happen much any more. Three or four days of waiting for the county plow is about as bad as it gets now, but for some that's bad enough. It is the old cabin fever stories and the possible threat that keeps us aware and in a preparation mode come November.

In this cabin neighborhood, which is quite remote, there are many stories of trappers, cabin dwellers, ice fishermen and sometimes travelers who have gotten weathered in for days or weeks and stayed busy teaching the mice to high-five. Or, like a retired trapper I heard about, spent hours one winter plaiting his beard into cornrows. When he finished, he would have a few beers, undo his handiwork and start all over.

There are several ways of dealing with cabin fever, a disease process of only human incidence that results from a traumatic confinement, usually to small quarters (read cabin), due to a protracted spell of bad weather. The wild creatures, being more adaptable and laid back, just snooze through the whole thing like the bears, who use this semi-comatose period of the year to deliver their young, go on a diet, dispose of wastes and other unpleasant tasks by tinkering with their metabolism. This seem to be a most sensible way of dealing with wintertime confinement.

Because major cases of cabin fever are rare now, it is seldom a big problem anymore. It is more likely to be just a matter of an unexpected snowstorm causing an unhandy, but protracted spell at the cabin. There were days not long ago, which many old timers recall, when, at least once a year, during a far north winter, one of those dreaded nor'easters would come roaring hellity-clatter over the Ontario headlands, pushing several feet of snow on a wind that could skin a beaver with its icy blade and paralyze this little cabin world with its few roads for a week or more.

This was a time for a real dose of cabin fever. However, we still use the term and apply it to all weathered-in situations, and the remedies depend on the will and ingenuity of the victim. One idea is to begin a Cabin Fever Box sometime in the summer. This can be any container that will hold information, equipment and reminders about all the projects you have been meaning to get at. For example, the average cabin contains over a dozen knives of various sizes and functions and they are almost always dull, so "Sharpen knives" is a note that always turns up in our box. Others might be a reminder to finally learn to play the backgammon game you got last Christmas, or to dig out the *Norwegian Made Easy* tapes you bought at that garage sale in Grand Marais.

AARP magazine seems to be concerned about the walls closing in on its senior readers, so in a recent issue it outlined some ways of combating the dreaded cabin fever.

One suggestion they offered was to increase your vitamin D level, not the sunshine vitamin, but the one which helps you make serotonin, the brain-generated good mood chemical. Another was to work near potted plants because they allegedly lower your stress level. Also, you're supposed to drink green tea because its theanine will help you relax, and don't forget to perfume the room with green apple or cucumber aromas. Beware of roasting meat smells. They are supposed to cause claustrophobia. I can't wait to show these remedies to that retired hunting guide who lives up the Trail, especially the one about perfuming his cabin with cucumber aromas while drinking green tea.

I prefer to spend some of my imprisoned hours baking bread. To me bread baking is more of an aesthetic experience than a domestic chore because it demands patience and creativity. Daniel Wing expressed it well in *Bread Building* when he wrote, "Each time I open the oven door and I see and smell the loaves, my heart jumps and swells a little." Bread baking definitely has a mood-elevating aspect.

"Here is bread to strengthen men's hearts," said the Psalmist. And a strong heart is right up there with a high woodpile on the priority list of the winterbound cabin dweller. That strength does not come from insipid supermarket slices, but the stout, hardy, no additives or preservatives loaves from the artisan/baker's oven. A bread machine will make a fine loaf, but it will only take about 15 minutes to pour the ingredients into the bread pan and the machine will do the next three or four hours' work. The process is foolproof but does nothing at all for the baker's soul needs.

When you are getting started it is important to remember that recipes in publications are usually only a guide, an average. It is possible to follow them precisely and still have a bummer loaf experience. That is because the ingredients are most often mixed and the baking done under consistent conditions of humidity by the same bakers using the same oven.

Every oven has its own personality and "375 degrees for 40 minutes" in their oven might produce an undone loaf from your oven. Humidity is also a very important factor in the rising process, as is kneading time. So experiment a little with the whole process. Ingredients are important but not chiseled in stone. If Grandma's recipe seems a little vague ("a skoosh of nutmeg, a handful of bran and almost an hour"), she wasn't putting you on. That's the way bread baking is. Some things you have to find out for yourself.

I think the big secret of bread baking is in developing the right "feel" for the dough. If you have a touch for fine satin, you have great potential. That's exactly what the dough should feel like when you are done mixing, kneading, patting and forming. It should never stick to your fingers, but should have just a hint of moisture and be a little slickery. This consistency is also described by Daniel Wing in *Bread Builders*: ". . . the dough is smooth, resilient, consistent, only a little tacky (not sticky), able to stretch without tearing and able to flow beneath my hands." If the dough is sticky, feels thready and a little like a wad of soaked paper toweling, keep slowly adding the flour mixture. If it shows the elephant skin syndrome with deep, dry wrinkles, add a bit more of the liquid mixture. When you think it feels just right, stick your index finger into the ball of risen dough. If the dent pops out after a few minutes, you've got it right. If the hole stays in there, you've got some more work to do.

Kneading is the stage of bread making where the loaf develops a life of its own. It becomes a warm, throbbing blob on the floured board and, like good sculpture, it evokes a tactile sense. You will feel a real need to get both hands on and in it. The dough hooks that come with most mixers do an adequate kneading job, but the true artisan baker imparts something of himself and receives something in return during the hand-kneading process.

If you are using a mixer, don't just dump all the flour into the bowl. Add the flour a little at a time from the cup using the low speed setting, because you are looking for that all-important consistency. The right point is reached when the dough separates completely from the sides of the mixing bowl. At this point turn the dough out onto a floured board and knead it gently by hand for about ten minutes. If necessary add a little flour or water to get that satiny finish.

Butter a bowl and place that nice round ball of dough in it and then take it out, roll it over on the other side and replace it in the bowl. This is to be sure the whole ball's surface is butter coated. Cover the bowl with a sheet of waxed paper or plastic wrap. Cover that with a cloth (a folded, clean dish towel does nicely) and let it rest in a warm place for an hour. Do not disturb.

When it has risen nicely, doubled in size, or just over the top of the bowl, flour your fist and punch the ball of dough down. It will partially collapse. Then turn it out onto a floured board, flatten it out with a rolling pin and let it rest for ten minutes. Cut it in half with a sharp knife and form each half into loaves.

Forming the loaves is a tricky step, and important, because it is going to determine the visual effect of your efforts, another pleasing aspect of bread baking. You can use the rolling pin to flatten, trim and roll into a cylinder, a method which most recipes recommend, but if it isn't done exactly right, that is, keeping the developing loaf a uniform thickness, it will be lopsided with a thick, curvy bottom seam and floppy ends, which are messy things to work with. The books says to stretch and fold a length of dough over the ends, but it doesn't work that way. A better looking loaf will result if you pick the dough up in your hands and work it, as a potter would a vase, into the desired loaf shape. Whatever method you use, you will want to put a symmetrical loaf into the pan because the heat and rising will magnify any carelessness and the result will be a misshapen, goofy-looking loaf.

Put the loaves into sprayed or buttered bread loaf pans and, with your finger, spread a very thin coating of flour over the top of each loaf. The reason for this is no great taste secret. You should put waxed paper over the top of these loaves before putting them in a warm place to rise. If you have a little flour on top of the loaves the dough won't stick when you take the paper off. If the dough sticks to the paper when you remove it, the loaves will collapse like punctured balloons. Let it rest in the pans for another hour or more and bake in a preheated oven at 375 degrees for 40 minutes. Then peek.

There are two ways to tell if the bread is done. If you have a thermometer, 190 F is the perfect temperature. If not, either use a long toothpick or a broomstraw, like my mother did, and prick the center of the loaf. If it comes out clean, turn the pan over, remove the bread and tap the bottom of the loaf with the handle of a wooden spoon. If it sounds hollow, the bread is done. If you're not quite sure, put it back in the pan and into oven for another five minutes. It won't hurt it.

You should let it cool for a half-hour before slicing it. When it has cooled to the touch, wrap the loaves in cloth. A dishtowel works fine. No plastic please, the bread has to breathe. After a few more loaves, you can branch out into bread sticks, carrot muffins and pizza crust. If the bad weather holds on, I sometimes get a bit overstocked, but the gray jays, red squirrels and deer mice with whom I share the storm gladly handle any surplus. Don't let cabin fever get you down. Keep busy. Head for the kitchen and bake up your own storm.

Cabin Journal Note:—
There is a very mysterious cabin here on Gunflint Lake. No one knows who owns it. Not many know where it is. Even those who do have never seen anything like it. It is located on a county road in very heavy woods with no access from the road or from the lake, between two larger pieces of private property on a little 50-foot lot platted over 50 years ago. If you bushwack down a steep, rocky hill and through a tangle of spruce, moose maple, old cedars, alder bushes and a thicket of balsam fir, you will find it close to the shore, but not visible from the lake. It is beginning to rot away and is mostly tumble-down now, but the general shape and interesting form is still there. It is shaped like a big birdhouse, in a cradle, hanging from supports, with entry doors at both ends. Neighborhood legend has it that it was designed and built by a long-dead architect who had an idea for an affordable cabin of unique design that was probably supposed to be very attractive to potential cabin owners. To any living memory it never was shown to that market or anyone else. Nor was it ever lived in. It just sits there rotting, reverting to the forest . . . another great idea that literally, never got off the ground.

Chapter 10

THE OUTHOUSE —
A VANISHING AMERICAN ICON

THE UBIQUITOUS AND EASILY RECOGNIZABLE little building out in back of most cabins and many older farms goes
by a variety of names: biffy, outhouse, privy and John are
probably most common.

In *Ode to the Outhouse*, a collection of outhouse
information with a forward by Roger Welsch, there is a
whole chapter on the derivation of the many names which
have labeled this American icon. *Outhouse*, of course,
refers to the little house out in back. *Privy* refers to a private
place, *Biffy* is allegedly just a corruption of the word privy
and *John* is a shortening of Uncle John from back in the
days when outhouses were called Uncle John and Aunt
Susan in polite society. Others, not in such common use
now, are *The Comfort Station*, *Rosebush*, *Sears Booth* and
Library. In the '30s during The Great Depression, they were
called *Eleanors* (a Republican jibe at the President's wife),
as the Roosevelt administration's WPA sought to create
jobs and promote rural sanitation by building outhouses.

In this neighborhood the majority of cabins still have
an outhouse. Almost all of the cabins have a septic
tank/mound system to handle indoor plumbing and gray

water, but at most cabins a little outhouse still sits jauntily at the end of a woodland path. Like a weathervane or a wooden-spoked wagon wheel, it's just nice to have one around the place. Or perhaps, the owner just wants a quiet place to read the newspaper.

There are many practical reasons for having an outhouse. Maybe the owners keep it because it is handy when indoor facilities are busy or need repair. In a remote area like this, it is a necessity in case of a plumbing failure in the indoor system. Then too, there is this matter of its infallibility. There is nothing to go wrong. One of the favorite outhouse names is Old Reliable. There are none of the problems inherent in indoor plumbing systems. In the wilderness context the outhouse is as much a proportional part of the cabin property plan as the cabin, the woodshed or the dock.

A couple years ago we had a family of weekend guests at the cabin which included a curious nine-year-old boy. As soon as he got here he hopped along the bouldery shore, picked up some quartz-flecked rocks, studied the big trees and watched a red squirrel negotiating a whippy cedar branch. Then he spotted the outhouse. He was fascinated by this little cabin in back of the big cabin with the neat cedar siding and the black wrought iron American eagle over the door. I took him up the path to the outhouse and explained its use to him. He tried it. "Cool," was his assessment.

I also told him that when they went up to Thunder Bay he should urge his parents to see the restoration of Old Fort William, where they have a big regimental outhouse with a line of 20 seats the soldiers called The Necessary.

Centuries before the days of the British Army, the Romans called their fancy, marble, multi-seated rows of toilet holes, the "necessarium," which was probably the origin of the British army term, which has now been shortened by British youngsters to the "nessy."

When they left, the young man shook my hand like a proper gentleman and said, "Thank you for showing me your necessary."

I am constantly amused and amazed by the creativity shown by owners in the design and decoration of their outhouses. Some of them bring the outdoors in by locating a large picture window across the front of their outhouse facing the lake. Frank Smith, a retired contractor from South Carolina whose cabin is across the Loon Lake portage from us, created a beautiful interior for his outhouse with wainscoting walls of ceramic tile, white board upper walls and ceiling and a large oil painting of *Mallards over the Marsh*. One of the most elegant outhouses in this neighborhood is down the shore at Rolf Preus's cabin. It is a two-story structure on a mound with a stairway winding around the outside and a crystal chandelier inside that really works.

Both Betty and Ron Hemstad, who live down the Gunflint shore, have a well developed sense of style, so they put off building their outhouse until just the right inspiration came upon them. They had an old garden variety outhouse for many years but a big cedar went down during the 1999 storm and crushed it, one of the two disparate events which provided the inspiration for a new and grander outhouse. The other came when their daughter Judy's job provided an opportunity and design possibilities for a new outhouse on the footprint of the old one and some unexpected but perfect materials.

Judy worked for a developer in Minneapolis who bought up older properties, took down the buildings and built new houses on the site. One of the houses scheduled for demolition had six beautiful old paneled doors with antique brass hardware which Judy took possession of. Knowing their interest in antiques, Judy finally abandoned her plan to keep the doors and offered them to Ron and Betty. With a gleam in her eye, Betty said, "We'll take them," and they brought them up to the cabin to make their new hexagonal outhouse.

The builder was Dave Seaton, their canoe outfitter son-in-law, who, in addition to making guitars, crafts other masterworks of wood often from storm-downed pine, birch, aspen and cedar from the woods around him on Hungry Jack Lake. Dave and Ron built a hexagonal biffy from the six doors and Dave designed a unique conical roof with a two-tiered ventilation system and a pale blue ceiling which suffuses the upper area in a soft glow during the sunny hours. The peak is topped with a jolly, antique weathervane.

Dave also built a beautiful bench seat laminated of multi-hued woods and made room on a woodside wall for a beautiful 3-foot by 10-inch stained glass window Betty had given to her daughter Nancy several years ago, and who returned it as her contribution to the outhouse project. Then they painted the interior a cheery sunlight yellow, installed a shelf which holds a Mona Lisa painting, and Ron added the final touch with a bright red, heart-shaped hole cover he made of a blowdown pine. The whole effect is more of a folk art monument than a humble outhouse, in its modest coat of forest-friendly, greenish paint.

One of the few necessities for an outhouse is a warm comfortable seat, especially after the first frost. At this time it is best to detach the regular seat and use a styrofoam block with a hole carved in it. To cut the hole correctly, trace the pattern for the hole from the "summer seat" on a two-foot-square, two-inch-thick piece of styrofoam and cut it out with a long-handled knife or keyhole saw. There is something about the porous nature of styrofoam that makes it always warm to sit on, especially if you leave it inside and take it out with you.

As the back porch has evolved into a deck and patio, so has the outdoor biffy of some cabin owners undergone a modernization and re-habilitation. The hole has been filled and sealed, the interior paneled, lighted and decorated with birchbark cones of dried plant arrangements. Often there will be landscape or wildlife art and a bookshelf installed along with a composting toilet, an electric incinerating toilet, which burns waste with 125 volt electricity, a chemical toilet, or some other "alternative" toilet. This is a neat and efficient way to solve the pollution problem, make the county regulators happy and retain the proper design proportion of the land-use plan.

Cook County Planning and Zoning folks allow the construction and use of year-round outdoor outhouses as long as certain Health Department requirements are met. I suppose they aren't allowed in more heavily populated areas, but the county seems to realize that in a rocky, remote, heavily forested area with no sewer systems for miles and most outhouses are used now only for emergencies or museum pieces, there really is no alternative. So they try to be helpful by printing a very clear set of regulations along with some nifty architectural diagrams for construction from the University Agricultural Engineering Section and a sly little sheet sub-titled *How to Keep Your Biffy Spiffy*. This is really a helpful manual for every outhouse owner, because it tells what chemicals to use to aid decomposition and minimize odors along with information on screening and venting and other helpful tips such as the recipes for scrubbing and disinfecting solutions.

In this North Country with its Scandinavian heritage, endless stories of the adventures of Ole and Lena seem to predominate. This one, passed on to me by a neighbor, has always tickled me:

"Ole and Lena had never been camping and they heard about a nice campground near Black River Falls in Wisconsin. Lena was worried about the toilet facilities, but she didn't want to use the word "toilet" so she wrote a letter to the campground owner. She remembered around Minot, North Dakota, where they lived, they used to call it the LC for "lavatory commode." But she was so prim that she didn't want to use the word toilet or lavatory commode, so she simply asked in her letter if the campground had an LC.

"The campground owner read Lena's letter and was puzzled about the initials LC. He finally decided it meant Lutheran Church, so he wrote Lena the following letter.

" 'I am happy to inform you there is a local LC located nine miles north of the campground. I realize this is kind of far if you are used to going regular. It is really a nice one, it seats 250 people. The last time my wife and I went was six years ago and it was so crowded it was 20 minutes before we could be seated. Some people like it so much they bring their lunch and make a day of it. It pains me that I can't go more often like I know I should, but it gets more difficult when you get older, especially in the winter. So you come down and stay at our camp and maybe my wife and I can go with you. We'll sit together and I'll introduce you to all the nice folks around here. After all, this is a very friendly community.' "

The American outhouse is, in all likelihood, an indigenous piece of architecture. Its function, of course, is older than history, but that familiar tall box shape with the peaked roof line and crescent moon or cloverleaf ventilation opening cut into the door has become strictly an American icon. Like so many things, it is losing out to technology but it will not be forgotten if the late Bob Cary of Ely, had his way. In his *Design and Construction of American Outhouses*, he says:

"It is noteworthy that younger folks have discovered the environment.

"They are seeking ways to lessen our impact on planet Earth. If it is located properly, the outhouse, it can be argued, is the most environmentally correct device ever developed for disposing of human waste. It requires no water, no electrical energy, no plastic or copper plumbing or sewers to overflow or rupture, and it pollutes no rivers . . .

"Those of us who are senior members of the society, elders of the tribe, as it were, with outhouse knowledge gained from long association, have a patriotic duty to instruct the younger generation in this important facet of rural living."

Cabin Journal Note:—

Everyone around here who has an outhouse has their store of funny stories about its use. Sharlene, a retired neighbor lady who lives down the shore part of the year, used to operate the resort there which is now in the third generation of family ownership, and in her day the resort was a little less modern than it is now. There was one tiny cabin, gone now, which was just right for a single occupant, that had a narrow little outhouse in back. A rather portly woman rented the cabin for a week and discovered, on first use, that she was a little too wide for the outhouse and she got stuck inside. She hollered for help, Sharlene came running and spent the next half hour tugging and moving things around until her guest was freed from her biffy bondage.

Chapter 11

Company's Coming!

IN MOST CABINS THE PRIMARY SOCIAL UNIT is the nuclear, or biological family, but many of them include the extended family, usually three generations of those related by blood, marriage or adoption.

The secondary group would be guests. For many, the cabin is where the owners do most of their entertaining, and guests come and go all season long. It provides the perfect atmosphere and surrounding for conviviality and friendship, the venue to share with friends and family. In their Travel section, *The New York Times* recently focused on this situation with an article by Kathryn Matthew:

"Nearly always it's fun for everyone," she writes. "A familiar weekend symbiosis in which guests bring extra life and laughter to the cabin while hosts provide a ticket out of the concrete jungle."

Nearly perhaps, but not always. Most people anticipate invited guests, but there is another kind, the drop-ins, whose timing is often bad. Friends stopping for coffee on the dock or to help install the new water heater is one thing, but those arriving unexpectedly with the family in tow for the weekend is quite another. Even though these drop-in guests are often disruptive, their arrival is sometimes our own fault.

Carelessly we might have said during a neighbor-hood Christmas party back home, "You're going up north in June? Why don't you drop in at the cabin? We're there all summer." Or, maybe, "If you're going to Thunder Bay this summer, drop in at the cabin. It's right on your way." The big problem is, that even though it was probably said with all sincerity at the time, chances are we will have for-gotten all about it by mid-summer until we hear those cheerful words, "Hi, we're here!" By this time, the kids are headed for the dock with their inner tubes, their dog is circling chipmunk holes near the woodshed and the grown-ups are hiking down the drive with suitcases and cartons enough for a week. We're stuck.

Because of our remote, deep-forest environment, there are some ways to shorten those visits. If the guests have a small dog, we might casually remark that recently several of them have been lost to wolf predation, and we always remember to mention that cell phones don't work here because there are no towers nearby. We make sure they understand that television is a sometimes thing because of cloud fade and the way trees grow profusely between the dish and the satellite. We have found that liv-ing without television is the core definition of roughing it to many city friends.

We are a little careful about whom we invite. Guests who love this wilderness country as we do are always wel-come, but I am surprised at how many people there are who really don't like this far-from-town, quiet, deep-forest environment. I can understand the kids complaining about "nuthin' to do," but some of the adults' hesitancy seems to be based on fear and the pervasive silence.

"It's so quiet. Aren't you afraid to be up here by yourself?" they will ask. My response is always, "What is there to be afraid of?" Certainly there is more to fear on the city streets than on a logging road here in the Superior National Forest.

Adult activities usually take care of themselves. Guests come up to the cabin for the same reasons we do: fishing, swimming, boating, hiking, visiting, cooking, loafing, canoeing, all those things friends participate in with us. The kids present a little different problem, but one which can be fun for them, very useful and healthy.

The cabin is a great spot for kids because they can play outside, something seldom done any more in their highly structured and protected lives, even beyond the electronic distractions of iPods and computer games, school, sports and other extracurricular activities. Also, apparently for reasons of security, parents are often afraid to let the kids out of sight for long, so they aren't often allowed to just play outside. But at the cabin in the safe setting of the natural world there is time and a place to dig worms, turn over piles of stones on shore looking for snails and crayfish, chase chipmunks, get their hands dirty, explore pine groves and shores, watch clouds and recover from what author/child development advocate Richard Louv calls "nature deficit disorder."

In his book *Last Child in the Woods*, Louv recounts the following episode in their family:

"One evening when my boys were younger, Matthew, then ten, looked at me from across a restaurant table and said quite seriously, 'Dad, how come it was more fun when you were a kid?'

"I asked what he meant.

" 'Well, you're always talking about your woods and tree houses, and how you used to ride that horse down near the swamp.'

"At first I thought he was irritated with me. I had, in fact, been telling him what it was like to use string and pieces of liver to catch crawdads in a creek, something I'd be hard-pressed to find a child doing these days. Like many parents I do tend to romanticize my own child-hood—and, I fear, too readily discount my children's experiences of play and adventure. But my son was serious, he felt he had missed out on something important.

"He was right. Americans around my age, baby boomers or older, enjoyed a kind of free natural play that seems, in the era of kidpagers, instant messaging and Nintendo, like a quaint artifact.

"Within the space of a few decades, the way children understand and experience nature has changed radically. The polarity of the relationship has reversed. Today the kids are aware of global threats to the environment—but their physical contact, their intimacy with nature, is fading. That's exactly the opposite of the way things were when I was a child. Not long ago summer camp was a place where you camped, hiked in the woods, learned about plants and animals, or told firelight stories about ghosts or mountain lions. As likely as not today a "summer camp" is a weight loss camp or a computer camp."

He goes on to suggest that "at the very moment that the bond is breaking between the young and the natural world, a growing body of research links our mental, physical and spiritual health directly to our association with nature. Several of these studies suggest that thoughtful exposure of youngsters to nature can be a powerful form of therapy for attention-deficit disorders and other maladies. As one scientist puts it, 'We can now assume that just as children need good nutrition and adequate sleep, they may very well need contact with nature.' "

Now cabin owners can provide many therapies for the "de-natured childhoods" of their young guests in a variety of ways.

Have plenty of young naturalists' equipment such as bug boxes, magnifying glasses for looking at butterfly wings and fish scales, egg cartons for keeping treasures separated, small aquarium nets, little shovels or trowels and a couple sizes of critter cases (clear plastic boxes with gated tops available at WalMart or most pet stores). For the smaller kids and rainy days, supplies like colored paper, magic markers, modeling clay, liquid glue and scissors. With an inventory like this you can keep the younger kids busy for an entire weekend. For the older kids, the following activities will be great fun, important learning experiences and will keep them busy for hours.

Who Lives Here?

One thing you might do is lay out a "Who Lives Here?" trail. Sometime before your guests arrive, make a path to birds' nests, chipmunk holes, owl, hawk or eagle nests, rabbit holes, rocky rills near shore where mink live, woodpecker or raccoon holes in dead tree trunks, woodchuck tunnels, fox dens, bark "bubbles" where tree toads live. Subsequent use will reveal more hidey-holes and give the trail a more used look, which will make it an anticipated attraction for the kids. Mark the trail with little flags at the stopping spots and have them locate where the critter's "house" is and explain their structure and use.

While you are making your Who Lives Here? trail, there are a few things you might keep in mind. Squirrel's nests are made of dead leaves, and raptors make their nests of sticks. If you see a really ratty-looking nest that seems to be coming apart, it probably belongs to a barred owl. They often appropriate the abandoned nests of other raptors or squirrels and are slovenly housekeepers. Be sure to bring field glasses when working on your trail. If you're near a mature deciduous woods, look for the nests of broad-winged hawks, grosbeaks and the dead tree holes of yellow-bellied sapsuckers. Forget about warblers. They are so tiny and their nests are so high in the trees you'll never find them. One member of the wood warbler family whose "house" is more easily found is the little ovenbird, the most common bird in these woods, who builds its oven-shaped nest on the ground and sings, "teacher, teacher."

If there is a black spruce/tamarack swamp nearby, look for black-backed woodpeckers (tree holes), gray jays (nests) and spruce grouse (ground nester). A star attraction would be an eagle's nest. They are unmistakable, always near the very top of tall trees made of large sticks and are usually huge because the eagles return each year and add a few more branches each spring. Some get so big they come crashing down in a brisk windstorm.

The larger holes in the ground probably belong to woodchucks, skunks, badgers or foxes. The thing to remember about foxes' dens is they usually have several holes. These are emergency exits and the den is usually on a little rise or hump in an open space so the fox can keep watch for a meal or another predator. The badger's den is usually found on a sandy bank facing south because the badgers like to bask in the sunshine. The little tiny holes scattered around the woods are usually made by mice, chipmunks, voles or shrews. Sometimes snakes appropriate these dens when they are abandoned. If there's a field or savanna nearby, you might look for the newly turned earth mound of the pocket gopher. Deer and moose don't live in "houses," but they have rest areas called beds where they sleep, nurse their young and hide from predators. These are easy to spot because they are usually a flattened out area in tall grass.

If there is not enough woodland property nearby through which to lay out a Who Lives Here? trail, you can outline an area about the size of a dining room table with stakes connected by a long piece of string to designate a microhabitat in which there will be probably thousands of living things; grasses, wildflowers, tree seedlings, forbs, arachnids (spiders), insects, amphibians, butterflies, moths and the tracks of small critters like mice, shrews and voles. Have them "create a small unknown" as author Richard Louv suggests in Last Child in the Woods, and have them explore it carefully. They are all a part of your Who Lives Here? world, too. You can make this encircled microhabitat almost anyplace in the yard, on shore or in the woods. Provide each youngster with a magnifying glass, paper and pencil and see how many living things they can identify and get on their list in an hour. You might offer a field guide to wildlife identification as a prize.

Natural Rambles

Rambles are short hikes organized around some specific goal or activity in the natural world. Betty, a neighbor with an artist's vision and an orderly mind, takes her grandsons on what she calls Pattern Hikes. On their walks through the woods and along the shore they search for the fascinating patterns that nature creates; the sprawl of lichens on rocks, the webwork of veins left after insects eat leaves, clouds, the mottled surfaces of bird eggs, spider webs or the endlessly interlocking branches of the beaver's dam. It is a good idea to sketch these things in memory and then try committing them to watercolor or charcoal drawings when the hikers return to the cabin.

In a little book called *Sharing Nature with Children*, author Joseph Cornell describes several of these activities which could be very useful when the younger kids get restless at the cabin. Most nature games make use of sight and hearing, but this one is a touchy-feely game called Grab Bag and it requires a little work before the kids arrive. In small plastic bags put a pebble, a pine cone, a snail shell, a burr, a feather, a milkweed pod, any little natural item you can find in the woods around the cabin. Blindfold the kids and give each a pencil and a piece of paper. Line them up and give the first one a bag. The child must feel the item for just a couple seconds, identify it by writing it down (anyone can write a couple words blindfolded) and pass it on to the next person. When all the bags have made it around the group, whoever has the correct list wins.

Cornell also writes about an activity that is not really a game, because there is no competition. In it, each youngster adopts a tree the same age as him/herself as a brother, or sister. Pines, spruces or balsam-firs are best for this exercise because they have sets of branches radiating out from the trunk that are grown each year. From top to bottom, seven sets of whorled branches will tell us the tree is seven years old. After the tree gets to a certain age it begins to lose its bottom branches, so the kids should be reminded to count those whorl scars where the branches have broken off each set as one year. The counting and aging of the tree will take the longest, but soon each youngster will have found a tree his own age and marked it with the finder's name on a ribbon or tape. Cornell reminds us that the best shaped trees will be found in somewhat open areas away from more dominant trees. The older the tree is, the more difficult it will be to determine its age. Have them study the tree to see if they can tell anything about its life. Does it have any fire scars? Are there any marks from a deer rubbing its antlers on the trunk? Any birds' nests? Has a new branch taken over where another has been damaged? When they have gotten to know their special tree well, they might even write a letter to it and then share with the others what they have learned about their new woodland friend.

This is an especially neat experience if the kids come back each year for a visit. They can re-connect with their tree and must remember that a tree grows from the tip upwards. The youngest part is at the top and the oldest and thickest is at the bottom near the ground.

Listen to the Sounds of Silence

Most of the sounds in nature are so soft they are almost inaudible. In the first chapter of *Listening Point*, Minnesota author and wilderness advocate Sig Olson says of his cabin, "I named this place Listening Point because only when one comes to listen, only when one is aware and still, can things be seen and heard. Wilderness sounds would be here, bird songs in the morning and at dusk. Aspen leaves would whisper and the pines as well, and in the sound of water and wind I would hear all that is worth listening for."

Some "sounds" in nature, like the butterfly's flight, are really not detectable by the human ear, and others, like the aspen leaves Sig Olson writes about, are barely audible. It is their proximity to total silence that makes them good subjects for this exercise. Perhaps this is a trifle subtle for the average youngster, but their natural curiosity and competitiveness is usually enough to make them try hard. Praise them if they do well and you will get an even more productive effort next time.

In *Last Child in the Woods*, author Richard Louv tells of friends who would listen for "the sounds they could not hear." Some on their list were sap rising, a seed germinating, an earthworm moving through the soil, an apple ripening, a spider weaving its web, a leaf changing colors. When the stars come out, maybe they will hear the silence of the day, the end of birdsong, or maybe an owl will call. To complete their experiences with the quiet sounds of sundown nature, the kids should sit still and listen for wild creatures, fish jumping, birds flocking in a tree, insects buzzing and frogs singing. Have them make a list of these small or unhearable sounds. You will be surprised at how many they will find in the magic of nature's silence.

Tree Bingo for a Rainy Day

You should hold a good nature game in reserve in case of a rainy day, and Tree Bingo will serve that need.

You, as game referee, will need to prepare a list of about 30 names of trees that grow in your area, and keep this hidden.

Each player will then use a ruler and pencil to draw a series of five lines across and down a sheet of paper, making 25 squares. At a signal each player will then start writing the names of as many trees as he can think of, one in each square, until all the squares are full.

Then you will begin to read the names of the trees from the list you have made. Do this slowly because each player will be crossing out a square when you read one he has written in.

Anyone who gets five crosses in a row, up and down or diagonally, calls out "Bingo."

There are a couple ways to adjust this game to your needs. If you do not have the required number of species in your area, you can reduce the number of squares on the paper to 16 by drawing four lines instead of five, and the other is to prolong the game by using other species: birds, animals or wild flowers can be used as well.

Let's Build an Inuksuk!

What's that? Inuksuk is an Innuit word that means "thing that can act in place of a human being," and is basically a pile of rocks, or large cairn, placed in a variety of shapes and positions which gave the people of the Arctic information about good hunting places, where springs are located, caches of food supplies, directions to take, all sorts of information they needed because they had no written language and there were no maps or other methods of communication. There are thousands of them in the Arctic which is an area dominated by permafrost and has few natural landmarks, so the *Inuksuk* was the only aid to navigation. In his book titled Inuksuit (plural) and subtitled *Silent Messengers of the Arctic*, Canadian author and archaeologist Norman Hallendy, who has spent years with the Innuit people in the Canadian Arctic, says, ". . . the Inuksuit are the material forms of the oral tradition. They create a profile in space." He says that after 40 years in the Arctic he can now travel all over the barren land of the circumpolar world guided only by the messages he reads from the Inuksuit.

From Wikipedia comes the information that an Inuksuk is the emblem on the flag and coat of arms of the Canadian Territory of Nunavit, and has been selected as the logo of the 2010 Winter Olympic Games in Vancouver, British Columbia.

Some of them are only small, gracefully shaped cairns of rocks a foot or so high and pointing out the trail, and others are massive structures shaped like humans, maybe guiding the hunter to the caribou, or it might be window-shaped, showing the way to some landform such as an island or a rocky ridge. Some of the thousands of Inuksuit scattered over the Arctic have been there for centuries. They comprise a prehistoric tradition that has been adopted by cultures on every continent except Antarctica, and many native American tribes have modified the Inuksuk to their own designs and materials.

Tell the kids first about cairns, the small Inuksuit, that many Indian hunting parties used to build as trail markers. Most often they mean, "I came this way."

Then, when they get the idea, have the kids devote a day to their Inuksuk building project. It might be a good idea to get Hallendy's book, *Inuksuit*, from the library and use it as a guide to sizes and shapes.

The kids must first decide the message they want to send, either practical or spiritual. Then, create the size and shape or texture of rocks which will best convey their message. A pencil drawing on a large sheet of paper would be good for a basic design to follow, then find the rocks and build their Inuksuk. Minnesota author and native advocate Robert Treuer, who has a large Inuksuk near the entrance to his home, says, "It is heavy work, gathering the rocks, bringing them to the chosen site, lifting and shifting them, arranging tiers and levels, defying explanation but ordained by the esthetics, shape and size. Above all each has an intrinsic quality, an essence calling for recognition and respect."

The lake shore would be a good place for it because there are usually boulders there, or perhaps in the woods or near the driveway. Building an Inuksuk has the advantage of longevity. In future years adults can come back and see what they did up at the cabin when they were kids. Combating Nature Deficit Disorder in your younger guests should be added to your list of duties as host.

Cabin Journal Note:—
The trail along the shoreline across the lake is the bed of the sad old railroad, grandly named the Port Arthur, Duluth and Western (PADW), but which residents called the Poverty, Anguish, Despair and Want. For years it struggled along carrying logs from the Gunflint area, ore from Silver Mountain in Ontario and occasional sportsmen seeking trophy moose or lake trout. It was extended onto the American side ostensibly to carry iron ore from the Paulson Mine at the west end of Gunflint Lake to the shipping docks at Port Arthur, but that whole enterprise failed. Only one carload of the low-quality ore was ever shipped from the mine, and a political science graduate student from UMD wrote in his master's thesis that, "There is far more iron in the form of abandoned mining equipment at the Paulson Mine site than was ever removed from the ground as ore."

Legacy of the Gunflint — Wind and Fire

MOST OF MINNESOTA'S CABINLANDS are heavily wooded, especially the sub-boreal forest of the Gunflint region within the Superior National Forest. Cabin owners are drawn to the great natural beauty of its rugged landscapes speckled with lakes and rivers. But an unfortunate reality is that they must be prepared to face the frequent high winds, lightning storms and wildfires that occur naturally in a landscape like this.

In his classic work, *The Boundary Waters Wilderness Ecosystem*, Miron "Bud" Heinselman writes that, "Virtually the entire ecosystem is fire dependent. That means that whether you are talking about pines, moose, mice or moss, they all rely on the regular appearance of fire." He goes on to say that fires have been sweeping this area since the glaciers melted back about 10,000 years ago. Even though these storms and fires occur regularly, no one ever gets used to them.

Near noon on the Fourth of July in 1999, our peaceful cabin neighborhood in the deep forest was literally blown apart by the Storm of the Century that caused destruction along a line from North Dakota to Maine.

Julie and I huddled, afraid for our lives, in the middle of the cabin under the central roof beam which we felt offered us the most protection, watching the trees thrashing and snapping in the 100-mile-an-hour downdraft winds of the Derecho storm (not a tornado as some thought). Loki, the big chocolate Lab, lay snoring indifferently at our feet.

It only lasted only a half-hour, but stepping outside into that devastation of whirled stacks of downed trees was heartbreaking. The driveway was impassable, with several dozen trees scattered across it. Two giant, old white spruce trees lay across the dock with their top branches 70 or 80 feet out into the lake. On the two acres in back of the cabin, nearly 200 trees of various sizes lay in jackstraw piles at crazy angles. Next door, Duncan and Ev had lost 40 of the giant white pines that characterized the neighborhood. A neighbor down the road who has a large property had a beautiful cabin in the woods, but when the storm was over it was more like a little house on the prairie. The storm impacted 477,000 acres of the Superior National Forest, snapping off over a million trees, and seemed to be more destructive in some places than in others. The effect of all that shattering of the forest on some residents was so depressing they left as soon as the roads were passable. In large part, what drew the families here and kept them coming back each year was the great beauty and solitude of this part of the National Forest. To look out over the storm devastation and realize the forest was changed for many years to come was more than some could handle. The younger generations who come now have little knowledge of what it was like before, and so have a different emotional investment in the new forest.

Perhaps the most terrifying and life-threatening of the natural disasters that ravage and reshape this boreal landscape are the wildfires which, prior to 1995, have burned vast areas of the forest approximately every 20 years. Since then the fires have occurred more often.

These fires are caused sometimes by careless campers who abandon their campfires before they are thoroughly extinguished, but most often they are the result of lightning strikes. Often the lightning will travel down into the root system of a tree where it smolders for several days, finally bursting into flame igniting the brush and trees around it. With the thousands of acres of downed trees from the Storm of the Century in 1999 lying like jackstraws on the land, much of the forest is a kindling pile waiting for a spark to ignite it. Due to the recent extremely dry conditions and more frequent dry lightning storms, there have been six major fires in roughly the same part of the Gunflint region in the past 12 years:
Saganaga Corridor (Romance Lake)
    Fire—1995—13,000 acres.
Alpine Lake Fire—2005—15,000 acres
Cavity Lake Fire –2006—30,000 acres
Famine and Red Eye Lakes—2006—10,000 acres
Ham Lake Fire—2007—36,500 acres
The 104,500 combined acres burned are only those on the American side of the border. Driven by south winds, these fires have often spread into the Ontario forests to the north, where they have burned thousands

more acres. Driving the Trail north of the Seagull Guard Station, looking across Gunflint Lake at the Ontario shore or exploring what is left of the Iron Lake Campground gives a sinking feeling and a realization of the enormity of this natural tragedy, but it is well to consider that these 36,500 burned acres represent only 1.3 percent of the 3 million-acre Superior National Forest. The charred skeletons of some trees will be here for a long time, but the ground cover will green up, an understory of moose maple, alder, hazel young birch and aspen is already growing and many of these scars will be healed within a year.

The reason for these frequent fires seems to be primarily the extremely dry condition of the forest in recent years. Wetness/dryness seems to be a cyclical thing, and hopefully we will return soon to years with greater rainfall. It is often difficult to remember that as recently as 2003 we were coming off eight wet years; and in that year docks were underwater and boats were floating off their lifts here at Gunflint Lake.

The Ham Lake Fire, which started on May 5 of 2007, about four miles west of Gunflint Lake, and was the worst fire in Minnesota since 1918, was a "renegade" fire, one which races off in rapidly changing directions on shifting winds, almost describing a circle, with the high, erratic winds carrying blazing brands which started new fires. For the first three days it was fought by 316 U.S. Forest Service and local fire department crews, Mutual Aid community departments, Canadian fire crews and equipment from nearby cities; helicopters, Beavers, air tankers, bulldozers, C-215 bombers, trucks, water tenders. On May 9, professional hot shot crews from Wyoming, Oregon and

Utah joined the fight and a mandatory evacuation was ordered by the Cook County Sheriff of the entire upper Trail area. The fire was finally contained on May 17 on the American side, and the total cost of suppressing it was 10.8 million dollars. 138 structures were incinerated in Minnesota and 347 people were evacuated. If the fire would have ignited and spread over this area during the tourist season, thousands more would have had to be evacuated and there would likely have been tragedies. As it turned out there were none. No fatalities, not even any serious injuries.

The evacuation went very smoothly considering the Gunflint Trail is the only north/south road bisecting the county. There were a few feisty residents who decided to see it through and not evacuate, but they were "escorted" out by sheriff's deputies at the last minute. All the traffic, emergency vehicles going up the Trail and evacuees coming down, moved along smartly with no bottlenecks. Larry Schei, one of our Loon Lake neighbors, couldn't bear the idea of leaving his big John Deere tractor to the fire, so when it came time to go, the Scheis packed the family SUV with essentials which Sue drove to town and Larry hopped aboard the tractor and drove the 50 miles to Grand Marais at top speed of 20 mph.

The storm and fires are memories now. The forest is renewing and regenerating at an astounding rate. Driving the upper Gunflint Trail today, the visitor will still see miles of damage. Great empty spaces growing up in raspberries, moose maple and screens of young aspen. Probably the starkest and most dramatic testament to the power of the wind and racing fire are the thousands of snags like those Bill Cashwell describes in his book *The Verb, 'To Bird'* as "trees without leaves, branches or even color." Not scenic perhaps, but the snags are a boon to wildlife, as we have 32 species of birds that use the cavities they drill out in this punky wood for nesting sites. The dead trees also provide insect-rich feeding sites for three-toed and black-backed woodpeckers and several species of flycatchers.

In response to questionnaires from the U.S. Forest Service, residents have indicated they would like to see more pines planted in the "new forest," so that is being attempted, but seeds and seedlings were destroyed by the latest fire, so it may not happen as quickly as we would like. In the re-planted areas near us, the new pines are almost waist high and healthy looking.

A huge threat to white pine survival are the deer which browse the tops of the seedling pines and kill many of them. Their presence here comes from an unfortunate conundrum. This was moose country before logging in the early part of the century. There were no deer here then, and perhaps they don't belong here now. From the turn of the century to the end of World War I, this country was totally logged and the slash piles burned. What came up predom-inantly was aspen and white birch, which brought thou-sands of deer in from west and south of here. They have co-existed with the moose for many years, even though in nature the two seldom share the same range. As the forest regenerated, the deer continued to destroy the young white pines by browsing their tops. Deer hunters love having the deer here, of course, and many people put out bushels of corn each year to keep the deer around because they are so cute, but this is poor ecology. It would help a healthy moose herd and a beautiful pine forest if people would only stop feeding the deer. But they probably won't.

From the wildlife's point of view, the forest is habitat, what the critters need for food, shelter and a place to raise their families. It was feared that the storm and fire devastation would so injure the forest habitat that there would be many critters killed, or they would force extensive relocation of the forest dwellers, shortages of food and other negative impacts on the wildlife. Fortunately none of that seems to be the case now; the wildlife population seems to be healthy and growing. It might even have been a good thing for some critters. The moose have reaped a bonanza of new growth forage and the black bears have fed heavily on the mineral-rich ash of the burned-over areas.

The forest seems to be under constant threats. Wind and fire are the things that come to mind immediately, but the experts tell us that the invasive plant species such as tansy, buckthorn, purple loosetrife, European reed canary grass and spotted knapweed along with the insect infestations of gypsy moths, weevils, tent caterpillars, emerald ash borers and several species of wood boring beetles pose a greater threat to the forest than global warming. One helpful thing people could do is to never bring wood into this area for heating or campfires. These tree-destroying insects often arrive in larval form in wood from outside, multiply rapidly and in a short time create a raging infestation. This is especially true of the gypsy moth which, as the name indicates, is a hitchhiker, coming in to the area in transported wood.

Three weeks after the fire Julie and I canoed across the lake to the charred Canadian shore and around the point into Oven Bay. What had been the busy little railroad town of Le Blaine in 1896 had been destroyed by forest fires four times. Visiting about this historic place, Justine Kerfoot once told me that she had stood in this same spot in 1936 after the big fire that year, and this entire Ontario shore, the bay and the ridge looming over it, was nothing but bare, gray rock. For us the bay had been a favorite swimming beach, a picnic spot, and a heavily forested place to hike while searching out the artifacts of Le Blaine's glory days when there were cabins, a hotel, the outdoor stone ovens of Italian bakers, railroad yards and a couple saloons on this ground. Now it was a blackened expanse of grotesque snags, stumps and glacier-carried boulders newly exposed to sunlight. It was depressing at first glance, but we learned to look more closely.

Here amidst the spikey, blackened sticks of a burned aspen grove was a patch of vivid green Clintonia, or blue bead lily, about to blossom. New blueberry plants, their tentacled branches covered with ovoid, fleshy leaves, were spreading across the lumpy ground. The faint trail into the burn is bordered with bracken fern, at least two-feet high already, three weeks after the fire. Along the shore, tucked neatly into the gravel and twigs of shore detritus, I found six loosely assembled killdeer nests, each with two or three green and black mottled eggs, the mother birds all trying to lure me away with their broken-wing staggering. The promising renewal of this temporarily shattered natural world, and its lesson for the human spirit, is but one of the reasons we keep returning to Gunflint.

Cabin Journal Note:—

All of the fire news was not grim. An occasional bright spot of humor could be found even among the dark clouds of the fiery skies.

Down near Hatfield's, across Dog Ear Bay, a crew of hot shot firefighters from Oregon were toiling up the ridge attempting to set a back fire which would hopefully turn the main fire thrust away from the habitation and people along the south shore of Gunflint Lake. Their progress was impeded by a mother bear with two cubs who wouldn't let them pass until they had made a pile of all their lunch sandwiches for the bear family.

At the very last moment before evacuating their resort on Gunflint Lake, Greg, Barb and the rest of the Gecas family loaded Moses and Jethro, their two mules, into a trailer and Brother Jeff came up from town to haul them to safety. After all, they are family too.

One of the Seagull Seven, who fought the fire protecting properties along Island Road with shovels, garden hoses and anything else they could lay their hands on, was famed chef and cookbook author Ron Berg, who with his neighbor Mike Lande "liberated" a threatened cabin's freezer full of chicken breasts, pork tenderloins and other goodies from which Chef Ron put together a marvelous feast for his fellow crew members.

And a little black humor. One of the neighbors, who shall remain nameless, is a neatness freak. Everything about his property is always spic and span and orderly. When he left the cabin in the fall, all of his equipment, even his sprinkler system, was locked neatly in the garage. That's where it still was when the fire roared through his property destroying everything.

SUGGESTED READING

A Place at the Lake, Paul Clifford Larson, Afton Historical Society Press, 1998.

A Place in the Woods, Helen Hoover, Alfred A. Knopf (Borzoi books), 1969 reprint by University of Minnesota Press.

Cabin Style, Jerri Farris and Tim Himsel, Creative Publishing International, 2001.

Listening Point, Sigurd Olson, Alfred A. Knopf (Borzoi Books), 1966.

Testaments in Wood, Wayne Gudmundson, Minnesota Historical Society Press, 1991.

The Cabin, Dale Mulfinger and Susan E. Davis, Taunton Press, 2001.

The Real Log Cabin, Chilson D. Aldrich and Harry Drabik, Nodin Press, 1928, 1964.

Up to the Lake, Tom Hegg, Walden House Press, 1986.

The Wilderness Cabin, Calvin Rutstrum, McMillan Publishing Co., 1961.

In the Strong Woods, Paul Lemberg, St. Martin's Press, 1980.

Cabins of Minnesota, photography by Doug Ohman, text by Bill Holm, Borealis Books, 2007.

A Taste of the Gunflint Trail, Gunflint Women, Adventure Publications, 2005.

Gunflint, Justine Kerfoot, University of Minnesota Press, 1991.

Woman of the Boundary Waters, Justine Kerfoot, Women's Press, 1986.

A Wild Neighborhood, John Henricksson, University of Minnesota Press, 1997.

Gunflint, John Henricksson, Adventure Publications, 2003.

The Long Shadowed Forest, Helen Hoover, Alfred Knopf, 1963, reprint by University of Minnesota Press.

Pioneers in the Wilderness, Willis Raff, Cook County Historical Society, 1981.

Last Child in the Woods, Richard Louv, Algonquin Press, 2005

Thunder Bay to Gunflint, Elinor Barr, Thunder Bay Historical Society, 1999.

Boundary Waters Wilderness Ecosystem, Miron Heinselman, University of Minnesota Press, 1996.

Boundary Waters, The Grace of the Wild, Paul Gruchow, Milkweed Editions, 1997.

Our Wounded Wilderness, Jim Cordes, 2000.